ADVANCE PRAISE

The Inclusive Leadership Handbook

"Donald Thompson and Kurt Merriweather have written an important book that enables leaders to steer through the intricacies of inclusive leadership in today's global corporate landscape. As a leader managing diverse teams, I've witnessed firsthand how the principles and ideas addressed in *The Inclusive Leadership Handbook* can create stronger teams and deepen innovation. This book will be a compass and guide for senior executives who understand culture's central place in organizational and personal achievement."

—**Timothy Humphrey, Chief Analytics Officer, NC Senior State Executive & RTP Senior Location Executive, IBM**

"Inclusive leadership turns traditional management thinking on its head by putting people at the center of success. *The Inclusive Leadership Handbook* is your guide in the evolving landscape of workplace dynamics and offers practical approaches to create environments where diversity thrives, engagement soars, and a new culture emerges— one that fosters lasting success and employee fulfillment."

—**Laurie Ruettimann, Author of *Betting On You* and HR Consultant**

"Embracing inclusive leadership is a moral imperative and a strategic business advantage. This insightful handbook provides a comprehensive roadmap for cultivating a diverse and empowered workforce that unlocks the full potential of every team member. It is a must-read for leaders committed to creating a culture of belonging where all voices are heard and valued."

—**Nils Vinje, Founder, LeadershipMBA.com**

"*The Inclusive Leadership Handbook* is a transformative guide that resonates deeply with our mission as a leader in the global home health care industry. The book skillfully merges inclusive leadership principles with practical strategies, essentially providing a blueprint for stronger culture, innovation, and employee engagement. The focus on inclusion and belonging is critical for understanding the needs and concerns of our greatest asset—our talent."

—**Rekha Daniel-Kimani, Head of Total Rewards, Diversity, Equity, Inclusion & Belonging, and Strategic HR Operations & Growth, BAYADA Home Health Care**

"*The Inclusive Leadership Handbook* is THE blueprint for sustainable success in the modern workplace. By focusing on people at the heart of culture, inclusive leadership becomes a game-changer, demonstrating an enriched corporate ethos by fostering well-being and belonging. Inclusive leadership starts with the C-suite charting a focused path through their organization, which unlocks better innovation, enhanced creativity, and resilient teams."

—Greg Boone, CEO, Cleartelligence

"As an executive coach and consultant, I have seen how the focus on culture building and creating strong leadership teams can lead to supercharged growth and organizational transformation. Filled with thoughtful analysis, actionable insights, and a well-crafted narrative, *The Inclusive Leadership Handbook* proves that inclusive leadership is more than an ethical imperative, but the strategic key to unlocking innovation, resilience, and unparalleled business success."

—Ann McCloskey, Managing Director, Accel-KKR

"As a podcast producer dedicated to celebrating diverse voices, I highly recommend *The Inclusive Leadership Handbook* to anyone seeking to foster a more inclusive and empowering work environment. This book is a comprehensive guide filled with practical strategies and insights that challenge conventional leadership norms. It provides a roadmap for transformative leadership, ensuring that every individual feels valued and inspired. Whether you're a seasoned leader or just starting your journey, this handbook is an essential resource for creating a truly inclusive workplace."

—Jason Gillikin, CEO, Earfluence & Podcast Ally

THE INCLUSIVE LEADERSHIP HANDBOOK

THE INCLUSIVE LEADERSHIP HANDBOOK

Balancing People and Performance for Sustainable Growth

DONALD THOMPSON
KURT MERRIWEATHER

Copyright © 2024 The Diversity Movement

All rights reserved. No part of this book may be reproduced in any form or by any means, electronic or mechanical, including photocopying, recording, or by any information storage and retrieval system without permission in writing from the publisher.

As you read, it will be helpful to have a notebook or journal available so you can take notes and complete the handbook prompts.

ISBN: 979-8-990-56700-9

The Diversity Movement, A Workplace Options Company
2912 Highwoods Boulevard
Raleigh, NC 27604

*Dedicated to my parents, whose sacrifice for a brighter future
allowed me to dream without boundaries.*
—Donald

*To my wife Valerie and four heartbeats Kayla, Miles, Ellis and Reese—
Thank you for the space and grace to practice and learn leadership lessons every day*
—Kurt

STRONGER TEAMS, GREAT LEADERS, and WINNING ORGANIZATIONS with *The Inclusive Collection*

Promote a culture of inclusivity, supercharge your communication, and unleash the full potential of your teams and leaders with **The Inclusive Collection.** From the transformative power of inclusive language to crafting branding campaigns that resonate with all audiences, these books empower leaders to build stronger teams, foster collaboration and creativity, and connect diversity initiatives to tangible business outcomes. **The Inclusive Collection** is your ultimate guide to achieving workplace excellence.

The Inclusive Collection is your compass on the journey toward a more equitable and inclusive future.

Unlock the power of inclusivity in your personal and professional life.

Order your copies today and elevate your team and organization to new heights!

Contents

FOREWORD By Alan King, President and Chief Executive Officer, Workplace Options xiii

PART ONE Exploring Inclusive Leadership

1. WHAT THIS BOOK TEACHES 3
The Inclusive Leadership Imperative 5
Self-Exploration: Building a Foundation for Inclusive Leadership . . . 7
Putting *The Inclusive Leadership Handbook* To Use 8

2. INCLUSIVE LEADERSHIP—AN INTRODUCTION 11
What is Inclusive Leadership and Why It Matters 13
The Challenge 14
The Solution 18
By the Numbers 20
Defining the Path Ahead 21
Exercises 22
An Exercise to Test Your Team's Inclusive Leadership 23

PART TWO The Framework for Inclusive Leadership

3. CAPTURING THE RIGHT DATA TO SPARK CHANGE 31
TDM Leaderview: A Tool to Measure Your Team's Inclusive Leadership 32

4. COMMUNICATION 35
Case Study 38
Skill-Building and Exercises 39

5. COLLABORATION 43
Case Study 46
Skill-Building and Exercises 47

6. CAPABILITY 51
Case Study 53
Skill-Building and Exercises 54

7. GROWTH MINDSET 59
Case Study 61
Skill-Building and Exercises 62

8. CULTURAL INTELLIGENCE 65
Case Study 67
Skill-Building and Exercises 68

9. RELIABILITY 71
Case Study 73
Skill-Building and Exercises 74

10. SELF-AWARENESS 79
Case Study 81
Skill-Building and Exercises 82

PART THREE The Future of Inclusive Leadership

11. INCLUSIVE LEADERSHIP ON A GLOBAL STAGE 89
Building Diverse Teams: Tapping into the Power of Differences 90
Authentic Leadership: Aligning Values with Actions 92
ESG, Sustainability, and Inclusive Leadership 93
Exercises 96

12. WHY INCLUSIVE LEADERSHIP MATTERS 99
Strategies for a More Inclusive Future: Sustainability and Continual Growth 99
Measuring and Tracking Progress 101
Inclusive Leadership: Impact, Transformation, and Beyond 102
Exercises 104

SUPPLEMENTAL INFORMATION 107
Appendix I The TDM LeaderView™ Inclusive Leadership Competencies 107
Appendix II 11 Tips for Leading Effective and Inclusive Meetings . . 112
Appendix III Build Better Hybrid and Remote Teams–15 Practical Tips for the New Workplace 115
Appendix IV C-Suite AI Guide–5 Actionable Steps to Spearhead Strategy and Implementation 118
Works Referenced 121
Acknowledgments 126

ABOUT THE AUTHORS 129

FOREWORD

Behind every thriving organization lies a simple truth—success is built with employees who feel engaged. My measure for myself and Workplace Options (WPO) is the answer to a straightforward question: "Are we helping people?"

Our goal is empowering organizations to improve business outcomes by securing a safe and healthy workplace that enables people to be their authentic self. The outcomes are significant—employees who feel valued for who they are. In turn, they are happier, healthier, and more productive. Each day, I want WPO to demonstrate the value of its customized well-being solutions in the lives of the 80 million employees who we serve. Our effort is expansive but essential, offering high-quality digital and in-person care across 116,000 organizations in more than 200 countries and territories.

Fulfilling the needs of 80 million customers requires flexibility and a deep commitment to helping people live better, more fuller lives. And, we undertake this effort in a world that is often under duress. At WPO, we support individuals through crises that run the gamut from traumatic events that are experienced by many people with little or no control, like warfare in Ukraine and Israel, to events that may feel equally harmful, but are only experienced by that individual in the moment. No matter the magnitude, WPO is there for employees every day, everywhere to help them face life's challenges, whether their needs are emotional, practical, or physical.

In the last several years, the world has experienced many traumas. We have almost become numb to watching them happen. But, WPO is not a company full of bystanders, waiting for someone else to solve problems. I call us "upstanders," which means making a difference in the moment. Someone across the globe is reaching out to us for support and we're aiding them, which is an awesome responsibility for an organization and its people.

For leaders across the globe, adapting to constant change is essential in building sustainable success. Recent history has been filled with transformative influences on our basic health and welfare, as well as new innovations that deepen humanity's connection to technology. In this era, when the basic premises of "leadership" have been shaken, the need for inclusive leadership is stronger than ever before. This is a people-centered movement, sparked by our evolving understanding of well-being, belonging, and productivity in creating workplace excellence.

The Inclusive Leadership Handbook does two things very well—first, it explores inclusive leadership as a foundational tool for creating organizational culture based on the core tenets of well-being and belonging. Second, the book provides probing and analytical exercises and prompts that will enable leaders—regardless of where they are on their career journey—to think deeply about sustainable business success, with an emphasis on the profound impact inclusive leadership has on employee engagement, teamwork, innovation, and revenue-generation.

As a managerial style, inclusive leadership expands and amplifies the talents of a workforce that feels psychologically safe, holds a deep sense of belonging, and has well-being as a driving force in their daily work lives. As a result, inclusive leadership is a strategic advantage that propels organizations forward, ensuring they are adaptive, resilient, and ready to seize opportunities on the global stage.

Unlike traditional performance models that prioritize outcomes above all else, inclusive leaders place their team members at the center of their strategies. This intentional focus creates an environment where individuals are not just cogs in a machine. Instead, employees are viewed as the heart and soul of the organization's success. At WPO, our goal in implementing inclusive leadership is to create an environment where everyone can be their authentic self in every aspect of their life.

The magic of inclusive leadership is its intentional ability to transform workplace dynamics into creativity and innovation. By valuing every voice, regardless of background or position, inclusive leaders unlock a treasure trove of ideas that lead to solutions far more meaningful than any that could be conceived in isolation.

As a result, managers and executives who want to excel must ask themselves, "How can I build and lead teams that can compete and win in today's marketplace?" When collaboration, communication, and greater teamwork emerge, then what follows is innovation and excellence that is embedded—basically woven into—the organizational culture.

At the heart of inclusive leadership lies a profound understanding of the interconnected relationship between individual growth and organizational accomplishment. Inclusive leaders champion a collaborative mentality, where the success of each employee is intertwined with the company's mission and values. By nurturing this supportive environment, inclusive leaders foster a sense of belonging that transcends titles and hierarchical structures.

As a business and community leader, though, I have even higher hopes for inclusive leadership's consequences. What I hope you'll take with you when you finish The Inclusive Language Handbook is the understanding that society has been fundamentally altered. Now is the time for leadership as a discipline to evolve along with the larger global transformation.

As I have traveled the world as CEO of WPO, I have talked with employees from numerous cultures and backgrounds, who hold a myriad of diverse perspectives. What unites us all, though, is the tremendous power of well-being on a person-by-person basis. At the precipice of this new era, executives must recognize this power and make every effort to transform the cultures of their workplaces—and the lives—of their employees.

I would also like to emphasize that inclusive leadership is not a political tactic, determined by your party affiliation. Inclusive leadership is not meant to exclude anyone. Instead, it simply recognizes that each of us are different, and feeling included is the foundation of personal productivity, workplace engagement, and organizational success.

Becoming an inclusive leader is the correct thing to do strategically and as part of our larger societal responsibility. The outcomes of inclusive leadership, including a deeper sense of well-being, belonging, and respect, are not just qualities employees want in their leaders, but the guiding principles that children want to see in their caregivers and we all want to see in our families and communities. Embracing this paradigm shift opens a path to a prosperous and sustainable future that will be made possible through the well-being of your most valuable asset—your people.

Alan King
President and Chief Executive Officer
Workplace Options
Raleigh, NC

Exploring Inclusive Leadership

1. WHAT THIS BOOK TEACHES

"Inclusive leadership is the ability to instill in others a sense of unique value and belonging in the organization or team in order to meet organizational financial and business outcomes."
—The Diversity Movement

There is a leadership revolution underfoot and the clock is ticking. The future of your organization hinges on whether or not you step up. Do you want to be the one who met the challenge or the person responsible for your organization's demise? The stakes are that high!

What we're declaring the future of leadership is "inclusive leadership," a people-first approach characterized by strong relationships built on trust and respect. Unlike outdated strategic management models that treat employees as incidental, inclusive leaders prioritize their team members and create opportunities for them to contribute their best work. The result is a two-pronged outcome that benefits the organization—a stronger culture built for success and a workforce powered by creativity, collaboration, and innovation.

Here's what's happened—the expectation people have of their leaders has changed in recent years. Much of the new perspective has been driven by disruptive societal forces that have shaken the world in recent years (e.g., geopolitical instability, economic uncertainty, diversity tensions, and global warfare), technical innovations like AI, and generational differences that have shaped and molded new ways of thinking. Quite frankly, what it takes to lead effectively is different than it has been in the past. As a result, a revolution is underfoot and has transformed the way executives must lead.

Every nation on earth is confronted with monumental challenges, while also operating in systems that many people no longer trust. Institutions that were at one time considered pillars of society are being questioned or even scorned. In this vacuum, organizations and their leaders are being called to play a larger role in addressing the world's most pressing problems. From every perspective, a leader's ability to establish and sustain culture through a shared set of values and beliefs that guide behavior will determine success or failure.

We deeply believe that inclusive leadership is the paradigm that will take executives and teams toward a successful future. Excellent organizations filled with inclusive leaders at every level will have a geometrically outsized imprint on society. The principles at the core of inclusive leadership—built and strengthened in the workplace—filter into homes and communities. What we have seen firsthand is that inclusive leaders take those practices into their personal lives, thus helping build more inclusive and equitable cultures, whether this effort is in philanthropic work, coaching youth sports, or work with nonprofit or religious organizations.

Inclusive leaders align the interests of their team with larger organizational goals, promoting a "win-win" mentality. The success of the employee is linked directly to the company's success. With culture being a central facet of managing people across teams and geographies, an inclusive leader adds value based on their understanding of the importance of diversity, equity, and inclusion (DEI) in building stronger relationships. Creating a culture centered on employee well-being and belonging fosters a more sustainable workplace environment where people feel valued and respected.

Let's not begin by thinking that inclusive leadership only resides in the C-suite or among extraordinary individuals who have some unusual gift or insight. Leadership is not limited by formal title, position, or pedigree. One doesn't even need to be part of what organizations traditionally deem "leadership." An individual can manifest the strongest attributes of inclusive leadership by building relationships, elevating the work of colleagues, and influencing others in positive ways. Clearly, from this perspective, those who implement the foundational ideas at the heart of inclusive leadership can have an outsized impact on their organizations and the broader society. Developing the inclusive leadership skills outlined in this handbook will help every person, whether early in their career or with deep experience, create a mindset built on trust, accountability, collaboration, and innovation.

As a matter of fact, we believe that inclusive leadership should be part of undergraduate and graduate business school curriculums, alongside ethics training and a stronger emphasis on the changing nature of managerial studies. Here's why: what we have seen through programs with hundreds of clients and tens of thousands of employees is that leaders who recognize the importance of DEI-led culture understand how it drives better business performance. Simply put, every future executive needs to know how shaping culture leads to stronger financial outcomes.

THE INCLUSIVE LEADERSHIP IMPERATIVE

The Inclusive Leadership Handbook outlines inclusive leadership principles, then reinforces what is being learned by providing opportunities for deep reflection. These tools, including exercises and thought/essay prompts, enable readers to move from theoretical idea to implementation, and may allow those that are dedicated to inclusive leadership to convince others of the benefits.

At this point, a reader may want to think through inclusive leadership's value proposition. While there are numerous ways an inclusive leader benefits organizations and businesses, the following six business objectives broadly outline its particular strengths:

1. **A Unified Vision for Success**
Inclusive leadership fosters a shared sense of purpose that transcends traditional hierarchical structures. When C-suite executives, board members, nonprofit leaders, and managers align around a vision that values every individual's contribution, their combined efforts create the environment needed for full employee engagement and buy-in. This unity ensures that strategies are not just top-down mandates, but collective endeavors enriched by diverse perspectives.

2. **Fostering Innovation**
Innovation provides the foundation for continuous organizational growth. Forward-thinking leaders and organizations are able to transform ideas into new business opportunities no matter where they are located. In the economy of today—and for tomorrow—inclusive leadership is invaluable, because it requires that a chorus of voices are invited to the

innovation table. The result: ideas, campaigns, products, and services are infused with fresh ideas and unique viewpoints. Diverse perspectives, we have come to realize in modern management and leadership, are crucial for organizations as they navigate rapidly evolving landscapes. A skeptic might argue that too many ideas may muddy the waters. In reality, leaders now understand that a diversified ideation pool leads to groundbreaking solutions—the kind that solo thinking rarely achieves.

3. Stronger Decision-Making

Inclusive leadership compels leaders to consider numerous perspectives before making decisions. One leader we counseled explained his deliberate intention to speak last whenever his leadership team brainstormed on a topic or debated a business objective. He wasn't waiting to pounce on bad ideas or play "gotcha" with other leaders, as leaders in past eras might have done. Instead, this executive realized that by inviting all team members to participate, particularly those who rarely spoke in meetings, the entire team gained by relying on one another's diverse perspectives in finding the best path forward. The decision-making processes for inclusive leaders are often more well-rounded and robust—informed by a comprehensive understanding of potential challenges and opportunities, and ultimately leading to more effective outcomes. This inclination is backed by research by Cloverpop, which revealed that "inclusive decision making leads to better business decisions up to 87 percent of the time."

4. Enhanced Reputation and Brand Loyalty

Organizations that champion inclusive leadership demonstrate an unwavering commitment to DEI, belonging, and well-being as part of the everyday work experience. However, the value goes beyond creation of collaboration spaces or campaigns to recruit new hires. s. In today's socially conscious landscape, consumers, employees, and stakeholders actively seek alignment with brands that mirror their values. Ignoring this shift exposes an organization to the possibility of a tarnished reputation or losing brand value, which translates to difficulty attracting and retaining the best talent. Leaders usually have a keen understanding of the importance of avoiding risk and preventing crises, but the idea that customers and employees are scrutinizing their companies from a cultural standpoint is new. There is no doubt that organizations are being evaluated on whether or not they live up to their mission and value statements.

5. **Talent Attraction and Retention**

Top-tier talent gravitates toward organizations that nurture an inclusive culture. Inclusive leadership positions an organization as an employer of choice, attracting a diverse pool of talent that can drive innovation and growth. One C-suite leader explained the value of inclusive leadership in building a culture of collaboration in their organization. By fostering teamwork and intergroup communication, ideas were prioritized, and as trust grew, teammates felt the psychological safety to ask questions, engage more deeply, and even dissent, without fear of retribution. Whether working to attract new employees or retain the most talented, this executive understood that a collaborative culture creates a sense of unity and empowerment that leads to smart decisions directly in line with the company's core values. This is the type of environment that the best employees and candidates demand. Advantexe CEO Robert Brodo sees the financial payoff as well, pointing to research conducted by the Australian HR Institute that shows psychological safe work environments "boost financial results by as much as 35%" and "improve revenue by 19%."

6. **Crisis Resilience**

The word "crisis" alone can send chills up a leader's spine, yet there is no central playbook for dealing with the kinds of issues leaders are experiencing (e.g., post-COVID recovery, managing branding missteps). Today's leaders realize that the ability to navigate crises hinges on adaptability and cohesion. By soliciting diverse perspectives and approaches to a challenge, leaders can anticipate negative outcomes, weigh a variety of solutions, and quickly decide the best strategy. In times of uncertainty, this approach allows inclusive leaders to make informed decisions that the entire team can rally around. And, as an added benefit, organizations that have prioritized an inclusive culture will most likely have earned reputational goodwill that mitigates damage and gives them space to address challenges.

SELF-EXPLORATION: BUILDING A FOUNDATION FOR INCLUSIVE LEADERSHIP

Successful leadership today enables organizations to capitalize on tomorrow's opportunities. Being able to balance short-term pressures and long-term possibilities hinges on open-mindedness and resiliency. By heeding the call to lead and manage differently, leaders will be prepared to operate successfully in an increasingly diverse and global economy. Inclusive behaviors such as cultural intelligence, relationship-building, and authentic communication naturally align with diversity, equity, and inclusion best practices. In fact, DEI training for leaders enables them to better connect with a broad customer base and amplify the talents of a diverse workforce.

When executives incorporate inclusive leadership best practices into their daily behavior, they give their organization a fast-pass to workplace excellence. The benefits will be obvious and tangible: increased productivity, better problem-solving, greater creativity, broader innovation, and an open, equitable culture where employees want to work. From the leader's perspective, some inclusive behaviors might take practice, but the effort will reap rewards. Along with the operational advantages, the business will also be better equipped to pivot and adapt in an ever-changing environment. Inclusive leadership is vital for sustainable organizations and the growth-oriented leaders who guide them.

PUTTING *THE INCLUSIVE LEADERSHIP HANDBOOK* TO USE

In this era of societal transformation and business evolution, the need for inclusive leadership reverberates louder than ever. To navigate the turbulence and achieve sustainable success, research firm McKinsey & Co. reports that organizations need an "approach that seeks to be open, fluid, and adaptable; unleashes the collective energy, passion, and capabilities of its people; reimagines strategy; and focuses on delivering greater value to all stakeholders."

The call for change isn't coming just from visionaries or management experts who understand the foundational role culture plays in workplaces and communities. There is a fundamental transformation underfoot. This is a people-centered movement, sparked by our evolving understanding of well-being, belonging, and productivity in creating excellent workplaces. Every leader—from the C-suite to board members and front-line managers—shapes strategies that filter throughout the organization.

Inclusive leadership is part of a new era where the last vestiges of "command and control" managerial structures are being erased.

Three Features Set This Handbook Apart
1. **Framework**—Clear explanations of why inclusive leadership is needed and context regarding its benefits

2. **Authentic**—Real-world insights from senior executives across industries and organizations globally that has been driven by TDM's client work with hundreds of global companies and tens of thousands of employees
3. **Actionable**—Prompts and exercises that provide valuable practice and deeper understanding

Use This Guide To:
1. Learn how inclusive leadership gives you a competitive advantage
2. Avoid the pitfalls and culture-busting threats of non-inclusive leadership
3. Discover best practices from inclusive leaders across the globe
4. Hone your inclusive leadership skills with thought-provoking exercises and prompts
5. Understand how to build an inclusive leadership ethos and culture-centric organization

What drives the modern global workplace is leadership that adapts to new and quickly changing cultural norms. Tomorrow's top organizations are going to be those that blend performance, agility, authenticity, compassion, and open-mindedness. Their leaders will embrace a diverse array of perspectives that exemplify the interconnected world. Driven by inclusive leadership these companies will establish teams that excel at navigating complexities, fostering innovation, and driving success in a multicultural landscape.

As a managerial style, inclusive leadership expands and amplifies the talents of a workforce that feels psychologically safe, holds a deep sense of belonging, and has well-being as a driving force in their daily work lives. As a result, inclusive leadership is a strategic advantage that propels organizations forward, ensuring they are adaptive, resilient, and ready to seize opportunities on the global stage.

The Inclusive Leadership Handbook is designed to inform leaders no matter where they are on their inclusive journey. By thinking about this topic broadly and working through the prompts and exercises, you will become a leader ready for the challenges of the ever-changing global workplace.

The book is meant to be used—literally written in. We've supplied space within the text for you to hone and sharpen your thinking, whether you're a board member, rising star, seasoned CEO, or a student looking toward your future. You may want to use the prompts as a means to jumpstart a deeper examination into your own leadership or even make them part of discussions with colleagues.

In Part Two, each inclusive leadership best practice topic provides insight into how to expand your understanding of the competency area as a strength, opportunity to develop, or find ways to improve in that skill set. Then, you are given thought-provoking prompts designed to deepen your comprehension of the area. Through this self-reflection, you will look at your own career development, but also how your work intersects with and builds on the strengths and opportunities across the whole leadership team.

Tomorrow awaits the inclusive leader who understands the essence of success in the global business arena. Get started today!

2. INCLUSIVE LEADERSHIP—AN INTRODUCTION

In a world that is rapidly evolving, where the heart of business success is no longer confined to spreadsheets and profit margins alone, a new era of leadership has emerged. Inclusive leadership is guiding the way forward, transforming organizational landscapes and reshaping how we lead and think about leadership.

Imagine a leadership style that places relationships at its forefront, where trust, respect, and collaboration reign supreme. Inclusive leadership is exactly that. It beckons leaders—aspiring and seasoned alike—to embark on a learning journey that promises not only professional growth, but also the creation of thriving, innovative, and harmonious workplaces.

Gone are the days when leadership was synonymous with command and control, when decisions were handed down from the top without consideration for those who bring these visions to life. No one has time for "cringe-worthy" moments or the shouting and denigrating that used to be commonplace in workplaces around the world.

One executive we coached remembered a meeting where he stated his displeasure with a beta product too aggressively, which caused the team to jump into crisis mode. The resulting confusion and emotional toll cost the company money and resulted in several stops and starts that led nowhere. Later, reflecting on the experience from an inclusive leadership lens, the CEO realized that being more empathetic in that moment could have gotten the project on track quicker and to a faster solution. How many situations like this come up on a daily basis at companies around the world?

Inclusive leaders recognize that organizational success is a journey that is enriched by the diverse experiences, talents, and perspectives of every individual on the team. They understand that the path to excellence is paved by valuing the unique strengths that each team member brings to the whole.

Unlike traditional performance models that prioritize outcomes above all else, inclusive leaders place their team members at the center of their strategies. This intentional focus creates an environment where individuals are not just cogs in a machine. Instead, employees and their sense of well-being and belonging are viewed as the heart and soul of the organization's success.

The magic of inclusive leadership as a practice is its ability to transform team interactions into creativity and innovation. By valuing every voice, regardless of background or position, inclusive leaders unlock a treasure trove of ideas that lead to solutions far more ingenious and meaningful than any that could be conceived in isolation. Managers and executives today must ask themselves, "How can I build and lead teams that can compete and win in today's marketplace?" When collaboration, communication, and greater teamwork emerge, then what follows is innovation and excellence that is an outgrowth of the organizational culture.

And, successful inclusive leaders are able to push the culture into the broader company leadership, thereby instilling a new vitality organization-wide. "When you tell someone they have the right, the ability, and the welcome mat to lead, even if they're not at the top, that's real power," explains Matt Sheehan, Founder & CEO of Exhale, a subscription-based home maintenance service company. "I share that because usually it's not the guys in the boardroom who have the best ideas. You have to give everybody that view: that anyone can lead."

At the heart of inclusive leadership lies a profound understanding of the interconnected relationship between individual growth and organizational triumph. Inclusive leaders champion a collaborative mentality, where the success of each employee is intertwined with the company's aspirations and accomplishments. By nurturing an environment of support, inclusive leaders foster a sense of belonging that transcends titles and hierarchical structures.

Inclusive leadership also recognizes that belonging and trust are impossible without putting DEI principles in action. Rather than an end goal, DEI is a strategy that complements and amplifies a forward-thinking leadership style. Inclusive leadership is a commitment to building a workplace that embraces each individual's uniqueness, where differences are celebrated, and where everyone feels heard, valued, and respected. In this space of belonging, barriers are dismantled and bridges are built, making room for collaboration that transcends the traditional departmental silos or boundaries. Considering the unique challenges of today's remote and hybrid workspaces, inclusive leadership's focus on teambuilding and culture is particularly helpful as companies adapt and evolve.

As you embark on your inclusive leadership journey, prepare to be challenged and transformed. Get ready to learn—not just from mentors and experts—but also from the diverse voices around you. This is an odyssey where you will discover not only the depths of your leadership potential, but also the heights to which your team can soar. Part of the "secret sauce" of inclusive leadership is that as you develop these skills, you will understand how to implement them with your teams, particularly your direct reports, which will help build a more collaborative culture. In other words, as you build these individual skills, you will have a comprehensive understanding of how to use them to create better teams.

So, whether you are a seasoned executive, emerging leader, or individual contributor, the path of inclusive leadership is calling. If you approach inclusive leadership in an open manner, willing to rethink old-school leadership and managerial theories, you will unlock untapped potential that is hidden in your teams. This journey will redefine your approach to leadership, illuminate new avenues of success, and empower you to create workplaces that thrive on the bedrock of trust, respect, and shared achievement.

WHAT IS INCLUSIVE LEADERSHIP AND WHY IT MATTERS

Inclusive leadership goes by many names and has been discussed under different monikers—compassionate leadership, daring leadership, servant leadership, and others—but the underlying concept is the same:

> Inclusive leadership puts people first, achieving business results through cultivating strong relationships built on trust and respect. By ensuring that every member of the team can contribute their best work—and an authentic sense of belonging—inclusive leaders not only accomplish organizational goals, but create space for creativity, innovation, and excellence to thrive.

Everyone wants to work where they feel valued and know they can deliver value as well. Inclusive leaders align the interests of employees with larger organizational goals to create situations where the individual's achievements are linked to the company's wins.

The link between people's value systems and the organization's mission have never been more scrutinized. When there is a mismatch between a company's brand value and its marketplace perception. Mistakes are amplified when every misstep can be turned into a viral social media post or an outright scandal, the stakes are higher than ever before. Inclusive leadership as a foundation of a culture-centric organization is imperative.

THE CHALLENGE

Being a leader has always required evolutionary thinking. Adapting to new market realities, shifting priorities to meet consumer demand, and integrating new technology are among the many ways that successful leaders must respond to volatility and disruption. This new leadership model is no different from the other game-changing forces you encounter on a daily basis. We encourage you to approach inclusive leadership with the same determination that has marked your successes and the curious mind that has set you on this course.

As we outlined earlier, global culture is changing. In past decades an executive may have had a mental model of their career unfolding in a fairly linear fashion, echoing their mentors, teachers, or coworkers. Fast forward to more recent times, and we are much more in tune with the zigzagging nature of careers, career paths, and the circuitous routes many people take, whether technology-driven or based on life choices. Evolution is not a straight line.

Skeptics might argue that inclusive leadership is just one more disruption, and that it threatens efficiency, requires excessive resources, and upends established hierarchies. However, evidence from organizations that have already integrated collaborative practices proves that inclusive leadership works. C-suite executives, board members, nonprofit leaders, and managers who embrace inclusive leadership are poised to steer their organizations toward greater long-term success.

As Valerie Keller, Global Lead, EY Beacon Institute, explains, "Today more than ever, companies are searching for a new genetic code that will help them continuously evolve—to survive and to thrive." Part of the evolution that Keller discusses is generational.

The economy faces two different impulses. First, the last gasps of a top-down managerial system that demands workers adhere to rules and regulations that make little sense in the new world. For example, across the globe, gone are the days when hiring managers could choose from dozens of desperate applicants. The demand for skilled, knowledge-based workers has tightened the market, and companies and leaders must intentionally expand the pool to find top talent.

Second, the youngest members of the workforce have been vocal about companies and organizations that don't live up to their stated vision statements. Young professionals are voting with their feet, going to companies where mission and action align. But, even more importantly, they are backing up their words by embracing brands that do the same.

Perhaps for the first time in contemporary managerial history, employees are firing their employers based on culture. As an executive or board member, you have to ask yourself if your company is doing all it can to prepare for this new reality. Rest assured that your competitors are.

Those who remain skeptical of inclusive leadership risk falling behind in an economy where the power of diverse thinking is a powerful determiner of where people choose to spend their money, work, and invest. There is no sense in hiding from change or thinking that generational transformation isn't on the horizon. Whether younger professionals upend the business landscape completely or gradually reshape it, the seismic shift is coming sooner than many current leaders think.

The combination of these forces—cultural and demographic—are sure to make inclusive workplaces even more valuable, regardless of where the company is headquartered or even if they have an office at all. Whether an employee is located in India or Indiana, the need for talent means they can be selective about where they want to work and where they want to shop. The power dynamic is naturally more attuned to inclusive workplaces as younger generations—now and in the near-term future—overwhelmingly choose to work for mission-driven, values-aligned, inclusive organizations.

Debunking Skepticism and Unlocking Organizational Potential

Change, for many, is an unsettling terrain. For the skeptical minds navigating the tumultuous waters of leadership, the concept of inclusive leadership might seem like an unnecessary disruption. They raise valid concerns—will it erode efficiency, demand excessive resources, and upend established hierarchies? The caution is understandable, so let's look at how to debunk skepticism.

Efficiency Under the Inclusive Umbrella

Skeptics often argue that inclusive leadership might introduce inefficiencies. After all, they reason, doesn't considering a wide array of perspectives consume precious time and energy? Research actually suggests otherwise.

Studies by leading management consulting firms like McKinsey & Co. and others have shown that the time invested in inclusive processes yields dividends in the long run. Organizations don't see culture-based work leading to endless meetings or convoluted decision-making. Instead, companies that have integrated this perspective gain in innovation and creativity, which is derived from more diverse ideas being presented in an environment centered on psychological safety. When leaders get a broader spectrum of voices at the table and in boardrooms, new and bold insights lead to better decision-making.

Consider a global corporation like Cisco, which has pledged hundreds of millions of dollars toward inclusive practices and has reaped the benefits of a stronger culture, consistently ranked as one of the best places to work. In its 2023 "Purpose Report," the company boldly outlines its goal to "drive positive societal change," stating:

> We are recognized among the world's best workplaces, and we continually strive to improve. For us, doing right by our people is not only a moral imperative but a strategic one. Fostering a thriving, inclusive, and supportive workplace culture is intrinsically linked to our broader purpose of powering an inclusive future for all.

In an era of skeptics with loud voices attempting to vilify DEI, Cisco provides a powerful example of inclusive leadership practices in action. The mix of practical benefits via culture transformation enables the company to break traditional barriers that hinder most global operations. "Our business has always been about enabling people to connect and collaborate across distance and difference," the report explains. "We believe diversity, equity, and inclusion is a core competency that we leverage to accelerate and amplify Cisco's existing business goals and mission. It is intrinsic to who we are—and who we intend to be long into the future."

Resources: An Investment in Success

Skeptics worry about the resources inclusive leadership might demand. In an era where budgets are closely scrutinized, concerns about diverting time, effort, and money are valid. However, viewing inclusive leadership as a resource-draining endeavor is a fallacy that obscures its true significance.

In reality, inclusive leadership is a strategic investment that pays dividends, whether focused on tactical implementation or strategic direction. Organizations that prioritize diversity and inclusion benefit from a richer pool of ideas, broader skill sets, and higher levels of innovation. This, in turn, fuels growth and boosts the bottom line.

At Cisco, the effort to create an inclusive culture is a direct benefit to success, not a financial burden. "We see inclusion as a bridge—a way to connect diverse perspectives," the company explains. The result: diversity initiatives that "spark new ideas, explore new possibilities, tap into the power of digital transformation, and inspire innovation."

McKinsey's Diversity Matters Even More report, which analyzed data from 1,265 companies, 23 countries, and six global regions, showed the interconnection of diversity programming and success. "Our analysis," the team concluded, "indicates a 39 percent increased likelihood of outperformance for the top quartile in ethnic representation versus the bottom quartile." Other studies have found similar results: Inclusive leadership is not an unnecessary drain on resources, rather it correlates with higher revenue and better performance.

The societal impact globally follows in line with these results. According to the McKinsey study:

> Across all industries surveyed, *more diversity* in boards and executive teams is correlated to higher social and environmental impact scores. Social and environmental impacts are also closely linked. For example, over 80 percent of companies that perform well on social-impact metrics do similarly well for environmental metrics. These relationships are robust and statistically significant across executive teams and boards, for both gender and ethnic diversity.

Organizational Structure: Embracing a Fluid Leadership Model
Skeptics often worry that inclusive leadership might disrupt established hierarchies, leading to confusion and ambiguity. The hierarchical structure, they argue, is a tested model that maintains order and accountability. However, the shift toward inclusive leadership doesn't mean the end of hierarchies.

Organizations like IBM demonstrate how hierarchies can coexist harmoniously with an inclusive framework, where diverse voices contribute to decision-making. IBM transformed its leadership model to embrace diversity and inclusion. The outcome? IBM benefited from a leadership structure that tapped into a diverse range of expertise, while also maintaining clarity in roles and responsibilities. Rather than seeing the new paradigm as a potential limitation, IBM used inclusive leadership methods to create an organization primed for the pace of change needed as a global consulting and technology leader.

By examining established organizational teams from an inclusive leadership perspective, a leader has the opportunity to find new synergies and break down traditional barriers. The emphasis on better communication between teams, tighter collaboration, and a commitment to better decision-making actually makes inclusive leadership a better organizational structure, particularly for teams that suffer from the limitations of traditional top-down leadership hierarchies.

Pioneering film director and producer Ava DuVernay, who was the first Black woman to be nominated for a Golden Globe Award for best director, described inclusive leadership as a wheel with spokes. The leader is at the center, but gains insights and strength from each person around them. The process results in faster forward motion, whether one is creating art with responsibility for thousands of people to work in unison or leading a multibillion-dollar organization with offices and staff at every corner of the globe.

THE SOLUTION

Inclusive leadership as a foundational management ethos is much more than a toolkit or playbook. Instead, it is a guiding principle rooted in trust and collaboration. At every leadership echelon, trust is paramount.

Inclusive leaders cultivate trust by valuing individual perspectives and championing the growth of team members. When leaders acknowledge people's unique strengths and contributions, the result is a stronger bond that sets a tone for others across the organization. When transparency thrives, then the whole culture is enhanced.

According to research conducted by workplace culture consulting firm Great Place To Work, trust is built on three attributes:

- Credibility—Do workers "believe" their leaders are "competent, communicative, and honest?"
- Respect—Do workers "feel respected" (both as professionals and people with personal lives)?
- Fairness—Do workers "see" the organization providing a "fair chance" for success?

This unity extends beyond the confines of a single team or executive. Inclusive leaders build bridges between teams, transcend silos, and form a united front. The synergy that emerges from these connections magnifies outcomes, as different teams complement and amplify one another's efforts.

Overwhelming Evidence for Inclusive Leadership
Let evidence guide your path, even if some people push back or view your efforts with skepticism.

Why argue what you can test?

In countering apprehensions, turn to the real-world transformations brought about by inclusive leadership. It is a fact that organizations embracing inclusive practices experience tangible benefits across multiple fronts.

The companies and executive teams that are having the most success in culture-building are those which have aligned the work with defined business objectives. The leaders at these organizations don't have a crystal ball or some magic talisman—they realize that demographics don't lie.

The future is going to be won by organizations that put in the hard work necessary to create authentic culture transformation. This isn't just a gut reaction, but what we have seen at The Diversity Movement, derived from evaluating hundreds of thousands of data points from client engagements and coaching hundreds of executives around the world.

Here are some of the most mission-critical wins derived from a workplace and culture built on inclusive leadership:

- Improved Employee Engagement: Inclusive leadership cultivates a sense of belonging among employees and across departments and teams. When every person's voice is heard and valued, engagement soars. A study by Deloitte found that inclusive teams outperformed their peers in engagement by 83%.

- Enhanced Innovation: Inclusive leadership is a breeding ground for innovation. Diverse perspectives lead to more robust ideation. Companies with diverse leadership are more likely to innovate and develop groundbreaking solutions, according to a Boston Consulting Group study.

- Greater Profitability: The financial impact of inclusive leadership is undeniable, stemming from greater productivity, higher retention rates, and other beneficial outcomes. Organizations with high levels of workplace inclusion are more than twice as likely to beat revenue expectations, as showcased by research from Enterprise Strategy Group.

Adopting and implementing inclusive leadership requires effort on the part of leaders who, for the most part, were never trained in its ideals. However, as organizations and their executives embrace the transformation, they will find that inclusive leadership enhances efficiency and multiples resources by creating workplace excellence. What we have seen over and over is that inclusive leadership serves as the catalyst for unlocking potential and turning small gains into huge wins. The transformation stories of Google, IBM, and countless others stand as testament to its power.

BY THE NUMBERS

Forward-thinking business leaders share the same overarching goals: generating robust profits and engaging employees. As culture takes center stage as a leadership necessity, executives understand that it takes more than great products and appealing advertising to drive profitability. To maximize earnings and minimize risk, senior leaders need to cultivate a culture where employees thrive and are able contribute their best work.

Positive workplace cultures foster belonging, collaboration, and psychological safety. These types of attributes comprise a highly-engaged workforce ready to compete and win in the marketplace across the globe.

But, let's not rest on anecdotes or conjecture. The numbers from real conversations and research with leaders, teams, and employees globally tells the full inclusive leadership story.

At a macro level, research by Gallup and others shows that highly engaged employees generate 18% more in sales and are 14% more productive than their counterparts where engagement is low. The key takeaway is a 23% increase in profitability. There is a significant internal cost savings too. Highly engaged teams demonstrate 43% lower turnover rates, which saves organizations many thousands of dollars in recruitment costs.

Below are additional statistics that demonstrate how better workplace culture impacts business results.

Revenue and Growth
- The 100 Best Companies to Work For® have a 3.33x greater financial return.
- Organizations with high levels of workplace inclusion are 2.6x more likely than peers to beat revenue expectations by greater than 10%.
- Organizations with high levels of inclusion innovation achieve 5.5x median year-over-year revenue growth.

Costs
- Disgruntled employees cost U.S. businesses $1.9 trillion in 2023.
- Leading organizations are 2x more likely to have seen an extensive positive impact on recruitment and retention. This could save U.S. businesses $1 trillion each year.
- Feelings of belonging at work are associated with over $520 in savings per employee per year. For a 10,000-person organization, this is $5.2 million each year.

Risk
- Workers who are burnt out are 23% more likely to visit the emergency room.
- Companies with high-trust cultures rebound from global interruptions, such as recessions and pandemics, the fastest.

DEFINING THE PATH AHEAD

The global pandemic caused a significant increase in employee stress globally. In subsequent years, people have been attempting to readjust to the post-Covid world, but challenges including geopolitical instability, societal divisions, and the climate emergency have only added to a growing sense of unease.

Recent studies reveal that stress continues to hamper organizations around the world. Gallup found that 44% of employees worldwide said they "experienced a lot of stress the previous day," the second year in a row that the number hit that mark. While anyone looking at the statistic would understand the implications, what the research firm uncovered is more startling. "Many factors influence stress," they reported, "But Gallup finds that managers play an *outsized role* in the stress workers feel on the job, which influences their daily stress overall."

For leaders aspiring to bolster their inclusive leadership acumen, deliberate training is key. Organizations that offer inclusive leadership training provide leaders at every level with the tools to create vibrant, equitable, and high-performing teams. Such training equips leaders with strategies to identify and mitigate unconscious biases, fostering an environment where everyone can thrive.

Furthermore, inclusive leadership training broadens perspectives, enabling executives to navigate cross-cultural interactions with finesse. Clearly, as organizations become more global and interconnected, those skilled in cross-cultural communication and understanding are indispensable.

EXERCISES

Reflections:

1. Think about a leader you admire for their inclusive approach. What specific qualities or actions make them stand out as an inclusive leader? Alternatively, what could a leader you know do to become more inclusive?

_____

_____

_____

_____

2. Consider a workplace challenge you've encountered that could have been addressed more effectively through inclusive leadership. Outline steps you would take to approach the situation differently.

_____

_____

_____

_____

3. Reflect on a time when you witnessed a leader demonstrating inclusivity. How did their actions influence the team's dynamics and outcomes?

___

4. Imagine you're tasked with building a diverse team for a new project. What strategies would you use to ensure the team's composition reflects a range of backgrounds and perspectives?

___

AN EXERCISE TO TEST YOUR TEAM'S INCLUSIVE LEADERSHIP

Leadership is not a solitary endeavor. Success requires a collaborative effort in which each executive team member brings complementary talents to the whole. Frequently, though, the team needs a leader who can put their own standing aside and look at what's best for the entire group.

- Are your team members playing to their strengths?
- Do their talents complement the overall strategic vision?

Just like an orchestra conductor selects musicians based on their unique abilities, a business leader must align their team's talents with the collective work they aim to achieve.

The exercise below asks you to reflect on how you and your team currently approach common challenges from an inclusive leadership perspective. The answers to these questions provides an introspective exercise to better understand your leadership style and authentically examine the strengths and capabilities of your colleagues. By considering how your actions influence others, you will gain the ability to fine-tune your approach, harmonizing it with the diverse skill sets within your team.

Innovation

Communication and collaboration are foundational for inclusive leadership, allowing leaders to build consensus in decision-making. Being an effective communicator comes with the ability to tailor messages that meet the needs of various audiences, making their perspectives feel seen and heard. Powerful communication lays the groundwork for better collaboration and sharing of ideas, feedback, and questions across the team. While all seven of the core inclusive leadership competencies play a role in the success of a leader or team, it's worthwhile to take stock of how communication and collaboration are present.

1. List the strategies your team currently uses to build consensus in decision-making. Is the communication clear? Does collaboration happen naturally or feel forced?

_____

_____

_____

_____

2. What would make consensus-building easier? What is standing in the way of effective collaboration? What approaches could you try (or try again)?

_____

_____

_____

3. What impact would better communication and collaboration have on your team's mindset and approach to achieving business goals? How might undertaking inclusive leadership development help make this a reality?

_____

_____

_____

_____

Trust

Reliability, self-awareness, and cultural intelligence play an important role in building trust between individuals and teams. Proficiency in these areas increases confidence—your team knows what to expect from you, which directly impacts their sense of belonging. Demonstrating self-awareness and having the cultural intelligence to address microaggressions also makes your team feel understood and supported, which builds trust.

The questions below will lead to interesting answers about how your team demonstrates trust, which not only enables your team to work together more efficiently, but also enables each leader to serve as a role model for their direct reports and employees.

1. What role does trust currently play in your team? Are there factors that increase or diminish trust on your team? Have you experienced missed deadlines, inconsistent communication, or interpersonal slights that erode camaraderie?

_____

_____

_____

_____

2. What strategies might be taken to increase empathy on your team?

3. If your team were fully aligned on vision and fully trusted in one other, what heights might you achieve? How would your business outcomes look different now and in the near- and long-term future?

Productivity

Capability and growth mindset enable you to gauge and benchmark your team's work. For example, if team members are new to a role or feel out of their depth, it can have a drastic impact on their productivity. Cultivating a growth mindset can help leaders recognize new approaches, harness unique perspectives, and ultimately create a more productive team.

1. Think about the individual skills each person brings to their role. Does work get done confidently, or are teammates still growing into their positions? Are your teammates aware of their areas of growth? Have they missed opportunities to embrace new strategies?

2. What could make your team more effective and efficient in its interdependent work? Do you see areas where the team is clearly lagging?

3. What would a strong, productive team look like? What strategies could be implemented to achieve this level? How might inclusive leadership development be one of those strategies?

2

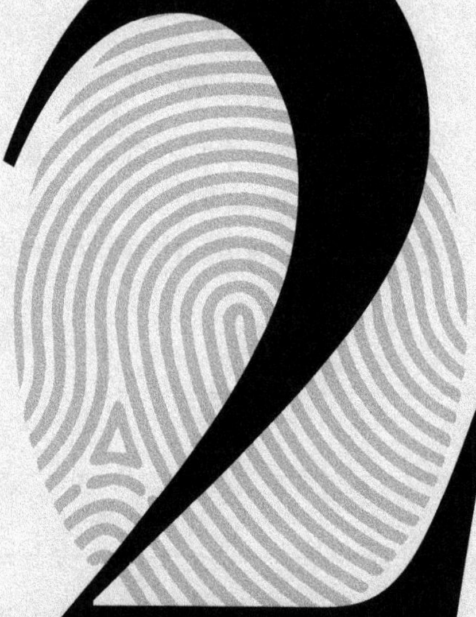

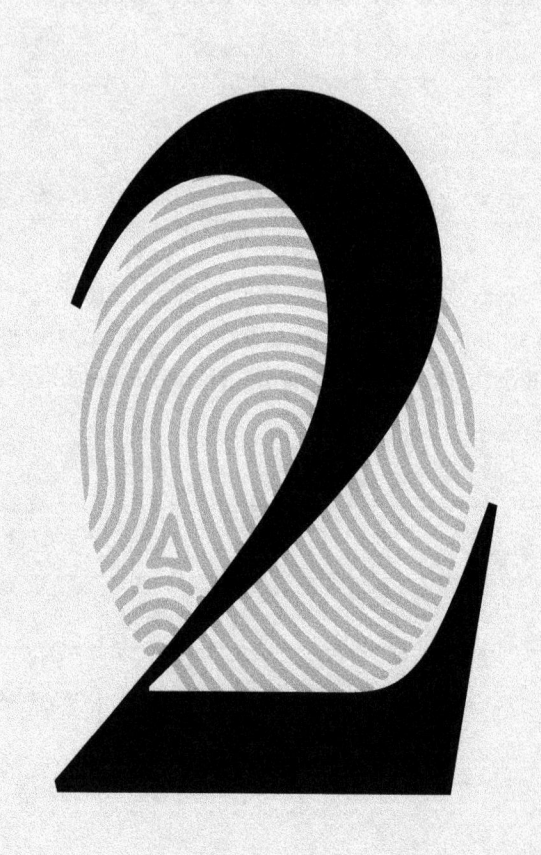

The Framework for Inclusive Leadership

3. CAPTURING THE RIGHT DATA TO SPARK CHANGE

Leadership ability can be honed through hard work and determination, like other skills. Anyone who wants to be a better leader can improve their ability via deliberate study and intentional actions. But, it's not easy or simple and won't happen through wishful thinking.

Growth and learning are impossible without acknowledging strengths, facing weaknesses, and being mindful of the impact one's actions have on others. Included in this type of critical thinking is thinking about your teammates and how your strengths and challenge areas intersect with theirs. It is not enough to just be an exceptional leader in your discipline. An inclusive leader understands that true *leadership* is engaging with colleagues for the good of the whole.

Similar to other creative skills—like a professional singer having a vocal coach or an athlete having a strength coach—both budding managers and experienced leaders can benefit from new thinking, as long as they have the information and benchmarks to understand their personal strengths and areas for improvement.

So, if methods to assess are available, what's the challenge?

The problem starts with objectivity and self-awareness. If you look at the career trajectory of a successful person, the list of accomplishments is extensive. The successes lead to promotions and accolades, often based on individual skills that are identified as exceptional. Leaders are then brought into executive teams based on these triumphs and expected to miraculously change their perspective from "I" to "we." During this pace of change, objectivity can slip into the background.

According to the *Harvard Business Review*, most leaders have difficulty judging their own inclusive leadership skills. Out of 450 leaders in the study, only 36% viewed their skills the way their teams did.

A formal, whole-team review process, as part of leaders' performance evaluations, can help create an accurate picture. In this feedback method, employees, teams, and colleagues are invited to share their perspectives. By hearing from many people they work with across levels of an organization, leaders are able to get a better understanding of their performance.

Third-party assessments are also valuable for leaders to get objective data about their current skills, shortcomings, and preferences. The resulting analysis can be a roadmap for leaders' educational journey; strengths can be amplified and weaknesses can be shored up.

"Leadership assessments are an important tool in the quest to get better as an inclusive leader," says Andy DeRoin, Product Manager at The Diversity Movement. "Using data and human insight to form and sustain teams is a best practice for culture-centric organizations. High-performance cultures are built by data-informed leaders who strive for excellence while fostering collaboration through empathy."

However, most traditional assessment models have focused on individual capabilities and ignored team strengths and weaknesses. In order to understand the interplay of talents, personalities, and perspectives that makes every leadership team unique, it's vital to focus on group development, not just on any one individual. Assessments with a belonging and relationship-building lens can help leadership teams enhance inclusive leadership behaviors, while attaining business goals across the organization.

Whole-team assessment tools allow data to be collected from individuals, evaluating their own performance and that of their colleagues. Then, by considering specific company challenges, the demands of leading a team, and how the team functions as a unit, the most pressing concerns can be identified and targeted. By relying on peer support and development, executive teams are able to realize exponential progress. No one person embodies every leadership facet, so peer collaboration is tapped to nurture proficiency. Strengths reinforce strengths, thus weaving a tapestry of trust and expertise.

TDM LEADERVIEW: A TOOL TO MEASURE YOUR TEAM'S INCLUSIVE LEADERSHIP

When your team isn't functioning as well as it could, your first thought might be, "How can I fix the problem?" But to get to the root of the issue, it's better to first answer the question, "Why can't my team work together?" The first step to a solution is gathering data to assess your team's competencies and key attributes.

Most executives are familiar with individual performance assessments, whether they go through periodic reviews, participate in 360-degree reviews, or engage in other feedback programs. However, most of these methods focus on individual capabilities and ignore team strengths and weaknesses. The Diversity Movement's inclusive leadership assessment tool, TDM LeaderView, focuses on the whole team's development, not on any one individual. Created by trainers, educators and certified diversity executives, LeaderView's peer assessment program is built on an **ACT (assess, coach, train)** model. The mix of skill evaluation, analytics, consultation, and coaching creates a framework to promote personal and collective growth.

Data is collected from individual members of the team, but the engagement doesn't end there. LeaderView also collects peer assessments from everyone on the leadership team, with each person evaluating their colleagues. Data is sourced from people who are directly familiar with particular company challenges, the demands of leading a team, and how the team functions as a unit. Results are analyzed to formulate actionable insights for current team objectives, while also charting an individualized course for future improvement.

LeaderView provides feedback on seven inclusive leadership competencies that are part of The Diversity Movement's inclusive leadership development framework: **Communication, Collaboration, Capability, Growth Mindset, Cultural Intelligence, Reliability**, and **Self-Awareness** [see Appendix I for definitions and more information]. Each person is evaluated in each of these areas, but the team is also analyzed according to the competencies.

Results are shared with individuals during one-on-one sessions with trained leadership coaches. Participants receive personalized feedback, guidance on what areas to focus on, and actionable strategies to strengthen weak areas.

Every team is unique, so leadership development strategies are individualized for each team and their specific requirements. Every team receives customized learning resources that help participants practice communication and improve their inclusive leadership skills. Following the one-on-one coaching sessions, facilitated workshops with the entire team continue the learning and growth by exploring how each team member can help their colleagues improve.

"The ability to grow as a leader through self-assessment and peer feedback is the key to progress with LeaderView," explains DeRoin, a leader on the team that created the tool. "No one person embodies every leadership facet, so each team member should work in harmony to establish proficiency. Strengths reinforce strengths, thus weaving a tapestry of trust and expertise. The data and learnings from the assessment are reinforced through daily practice to amplify communication, collaboration, trust, and efficiency."

Great leadership isn't knowing all the answers; it's knowing how to supercharge the collective power of the team and getting the data to challenge assumptions. Rather than assuming what their team needs, inclusive leaders collect meaningful data that inform actionable strategies to break down silos, boost performance, and drive organizational wins.

The inclusive leadership competencies—Communication, Collaboration, Capability, Growth Mindset, Cultural Intelligence, Reliability, and Self-Awareness—form a valuable framework when considering the strengths and challenges of senior leaders and their teams.

A single leader doesn't always have to be the person with the answers. Organizations can rely on the collective genius of their teams to innovate and solve challenges. Using a data-driven approach, leaders can navigate change, develop a culture of collaboration, enhance productivity, and cultivate a welcoming workplace where everyone can do their best work.

Inclusive Leadership Core Competencies

- Communication
- Collaboration
- Capability
- Growth Mindset
- Cultural Intelligence
- Reliability
- Self-Awareness

4. COMMUNICATION

Executive teams succeed or fail based on communication. At the heart of success is a culture of candor, which enables stronger relationships, collaborative teamwork across function areas, and getting to critical conversations faster and more efficiently.

Better communication skills enable leaders to engage with stakeholders organization-wide, leading to communication that is persuasive, inspiring, and clear. Credible and authentic communication also nurtures trust, speeding up the adoption of new ideas and strengthening teams. Conversations are authentic and transparent, and before making decisions, inclusive leaders listen to many perspectives. Communication is the cornerstone for creating a collaborative culture that embraces critical feedback and enables teams to achieve better outcomes faster.

This powerful leadership essential helps prevent misunderstandings and resolve conflicts. Active listening, a vital component of communication, enables a deeper understanding of contexts and situations. Effective communicators listen attentively, respond thoughtfully, and are skilled at finding solutions. When people communicate well, they are able to gain a holistic view of the problem, enabling long-term solutions, not just quick fixes.

In the business world, clear, reliable communication is essential to understand and meet customers' needs. Building trust and nurturing positive customer relationships is paramount. Communication with customers includes everything from responding to complaints to crafting Instagram posts to publishing email newsletters. Organizations build brand loyalty through authentic, intentional communication.

In today's dynamic and diverse business landscape, effective communication is vital for successful leadership teams. By mastering this key capability, leaders can cultivate diverse teams, which can in turn, demonstrate the innovative thinking and agile decision-making necessary to meet present and future challenges. However, communication involves more than crafting a persuasive message or telling people what to do. The multifaceted skill is demonstrated in the following key leadership practices:

Investing in relationships: Inclusive leaders use their communication skills to build relationships with their team members, colleagues in other departments, C-suite executives, peers and connections in other companies or industries, friends, family and acquaintances. They approach every interaction with an open mind and a willingness to listen and learn. They use inclusive language that shows respect for others and a commitment to honor their individuality. This capacity to build partnerships and form coalitions can drive positive change—whether it's launching a new product within your organization or serving the larger community.

Setting clear expectations: Leading teams effectively requires setting clear expectations and explaining them with clarity and economy. But good workplace communication doesn't end there. Inclusive leaders check for understanding, asking questions to make sure everyone is aligned. They are aware of each person's preferred method of communication, and they use multiple platforms—text, email, phone, or video call—to ensure that their message is understood. Inclusive leaders also make sure the decision-making process includes diverse perspectives from everyone involved.

Demonstrating authenticity: Honesty, vulnerability, and trust are the hallmarks of an inclusive leader's communication style. They provide feedback with integrity and candor, and they expect others to respond in kind. These honest and open conversations strengthen relationships and encourage collaboration within teams and across departments. Inclusive leaders are willing to share personal experiences that demonstrate their empathy with others. These authentic stories also reveal the leader's motivations, perspectives, and priorities.

Practicing patience: Some people need or want time to process their thoughts before sharing, while others have had years of practice speaking off the cuff. Trained communicators can be challenged by people who are long-winded, speak in a narrative fashion, or take more time to process their thoughts. Strong communicators practice patience and also ask questions to clarify and tease out nuances from those who may be slow or reluctant communicators. "Tell me more" is one of the most useful phrases for inclusive leaders. Be open to different styles of communication that allow others to share ideas, such as email, text, or one-on-one conversations.

Listening with intent: Active listening is a hallmark of strong communication. Give the other person your undivided attention, summarize their statements, and ask questions to gain clarity. Recognize the value of diverse viewpoints in sparking innovation, and create opportunities for every team member to share their ideas, perspectives, and concerns.

Sharon Delaney McCloud, Director of Corporate Communications at UNC Health, is an Emmy Award-winning broadcaster, TEDx Speaker, Certified Diversity Executive®, executive coach, author, and communications practitioner. Her advice begins with one of the most fundamental aspects of inclusive leadership—listening with intention.

"Making time to hear another person's perspective shows that you value their opinion, and it also enables you to see challenges and opportunities in new ways," she explains. "Active listening enables us to move beyond hearing just words, to understanding the full message being conveyed, which may be communicated via tone and nonverbal cues."

Learning inclusive listening: Inclusive listening entails intentionally listening to the voices of a diverse workforce. In a global workforce where English may not be the first language, inclusive listening incorporates the ability to understand different accents. Research has shown that accents can make speech more challenging to process, which may lead to memory lapses, snap judgments, and doubts about the speaker's credibility. These biases can impair communication, so it's crucial to tune your ear to different accents or unfamiliar speech patterns. Inclusive listening also requires compassion. Eliminating phrases like, "What?" or "I didn't understand you," is essential, since these phrases inadvertently place blame. Instead, take responsibility for what you are hearing by using phrases like, "I'm sorry. Can you repeat that for me?"

Watching body language: Body language may convey unspoken messages. Observe cues, such as a furrowed brow, crossed arms, or slumped shoulders, which may indicate concern, defensiveness, or defeat, respectively. Keep in mind that different cultures have unique norms and interpretations of body language. What may be considered polite or respectful in one culture might be seen as offensive or inappropriate in another. For example, making direct eye contact is viewed as a sign of attentiveness in some cultures, but as a challenge or rudeness in others. Ignoring these differences can lead to misunderstandings and conflicts in globally diverse workplaces.

CASE STUDY

Before **Dan Martin**, Vice President of Marketing for DHI Group, joined the company's Pride employee resource group as its executive sponsor, he thought he understood the challenges of the LGBTQ+ community. But, as he listened to individuals describe the obstacles they faced at work and the emotional turmoil caused by anti-LGBTQ+ legislation, he realized how much he didn't know. He also realized that DHI could do more to support its LGBTQ+ employees. He explains:

> Early in my career, a mentor said something to me that I will always remember: "Everyone deserves the chance to have a decent day." At the time, it seemed like such a low bar, but looking at it now, it's still more of a dream than a reality. I've always considered myself an advocate and an ally, and in recent years, I've realized that I was spending too much time on the sidelines instead of truly joining in the fight.
>
> My revelation came when I heard a similar sentiment from a member of our Pride Group: "We are human beings just like everyone else, and we just want to live our lives in peace." My heart broke to hear that plea and to see all of the heads nodding along in our meeting. That should be something achievable, and it's what I'll be fighting for until we can get there.

Martin used these experiences to expand the conversation on LGBTQ+ topics, and then took action. Using inclusive leadership practices, he and his teammates sponsored changes to the company's health plan, as well as company-wide educational programming. He led an effort to expand the organization's engagement, saying:

> During Pride Month this year, we were able to organize events at all of our locations. As a special surprise this year, we brought in a drag queen to perform in our Denver office. In addition to many employees who attended live, we had more than 100 dial in virtually. The performance was nothing short of world-class. In addition to her dance routines, Fonda shared the history of drag to a captive audience, focusing on its importance to the LGBTQ+ community and the deep meaning it holds both for those who

participate and those who enjoy it. It was an incredibly powerful discussion on community and humanity.

After the session, a member of our Pride Group told me that she had never felt more supported, valued, and celebrated than she had working at DHI Group, Inc. She also said she turned down three different higher-paying job offers, because feeling safe in a culture that's inclusive and understanding is more important. The business impact of DEIB efforts should never be the first thing we think about as leaders. That said, there's no better example of it than an interaction like this.

SKILL-BUILDING AND EXERCISES

Communication can be a challenge, even for very successful people, however it is a skill that can be improved with practice and self-awareness. The key is to always strive to understand other people and their lived experiences, because inclusive leaders see every conversation as an opportunity to learn something new. Even if you're an adept communicator, there is always room to grow.

Communication as a personal strength: Meetings are a common communication venue, and as a strong communicator, you can ensure they progress efficiently and inclusively [*see* Appendix II for more on inclusive meetings]. First, send out agendas and any reading material before the meeting, which ensures that attendees have time to prepare their thoughts. At the meeting, give everyone an opportunity to contribute. If some individuals aren't speaking, ask them a question related to their expertise, such as "Brenda, does that timeline seem reasonable to you?" At the end of every meeting, leave time for final comments. If someone is reluctant to speak in a group, follow up one-on-one or encourage them to submit written comments. After the meeting, send out a list of key discussion items, action items, and next steps. That way, priorities are clear and those unable to attend the meeting won't miss important information.

Communication as a personal area of opportunity: Practice and preparation are essential for effective communication. You have to know what you want to say and how you are going to say it. To best convey your message, plan your communication from start to finish, taking into account potential questions, objections, or alternate perspectives that may come up during the conversation. Think through your responses, so you can address any concerns calmly, accurately, and with confidence. When communicating with a group, identify what would resonate with them personally.

How you convey a message is just as important as the message itself. If you're announcing an exciting new project, but deliver the news in a monotone, your audience is likely to feel indifferent at best. Monitor your tone in any message, considering volume, projection, intonation, and word choice. Written communication, like email and texts in particular, can be misinterpreted, so follow up verbally if possible to ensure clarity.

Communication as a team area of opportunity: One of the best ways to immediately improve team communication is to prioritize inclusive language, by adopting practices, such as those outlined in *The Inclusive Language Handbook* by TDM Co-founder Jackie Ferguson. Inclusive language can bridge cultural divides and improve your team's sense of day-to-day belonging. Inclusive language best practices include using people-first language, avoiding jargon and acronyms, and eliminating biased language and microaggressions. If you hear someone use non-inclusive language, gently correct them. By using inclusive language yourself, and encouraging others to do the same, you can help break down communication barriers.

Reflections

1. Consider an example of poor communication at your organization. What happened? What were the repercussions?

_____

_____

_____

_____

2. When you think about moments when communication efforts worked or faltered, ask yourself the following questions to gain clarity. How could effective communication have made a difference in the success of the program, campaign, or project? How might better communication have sped up the adoption of new ideas?

_____

_____

3. Do you have a preferred way of communicating? If you're more comfortable expressing yourself in writing, you can grow your skills by signing up for a public speaking course or volunteering to speak in a public forum. If you can happily speak extemporaneously, but writing is a challenge, offer to contribute a blog post or article on a favorite topic.

5. COLLABORATION

Organizations face constant change, and creating winning teams is key to meeting the challenges of today's volatile global economy. Unlike a group of individuals attempting to go it alone, strong cohesive teams have access to data that goes beyond what one person can know. This enables leaders to tap into diverse viewpoints, exponentially increasing the impact of each person. A collaborative culture not only invites others to participate in idea generation, but also encourages questions, dialogue, and even dissent.

At the executive level, collaborative leaders understand that a unified team is key to effective decision-making and upholding an organization's core values. Executive leadership teams are increasingly focused on sustainable growth, which relies on "networked leadership teams [to] steer the organization," according to a report on the future of leadership from McKinsey. However, a persistent challenge for executives is to create an environment where better teamwork is organic.

"The old hierarchical model of leadership is increasingly seen as an obstacle to meeting the complex demands facing today's organizations," the report states. "Companies seeking to thrive now still need leaders who are accountable for their individual roles—but leadership itself resides in the teams of leaders acting in service to the organization."

In many organizations, you're likely to find a leadership team with a Chief Operating Officer (COO), Chief Human Resources Officer (CHRO), Chief Financial Officer (CFO), and other functional leaders. While each member of the C-suite has their own function, it's vital that they all come together to identify and articulate what they're trying to accomplish as a team. Establishing a common set of goals creates team alignment and allows their actions to be more naturally coordinated and amplified.

Truly collaborative leaders nurture psychologically safe workplaces where ambiguity is not feared and conflicting ideas are welcomed. Within this safe space, diverse talents are cultivated through open-mindedness and active listening, reinforcing a profound sense of belonging and individual contribution to the team's collective mission.

Workplace Options (WPO) is the world's largest independent provider of holistic well-being solutions. Through customized programs and a comprehensive global network of credentialed providers and professionals, WPO supports individuals to become healthier, happier, and more productive both personally and professionally. Trusted by 56 percent of Fortune 500 companies, WPO delivers high-quality care digitally and in-person to more than 80 million people across 116,000 organizations in more than 200 countries and territories and is headquartered in Raleigh, North Carolina.

Alan King, WPO President and CEO, helps organizations understand the distinct tie between workplace well-being and inclusive leadership. His advice is for executives to create environments where everyone can share their honest input without fear of retaliation, criticism, or ridicule.

"Psychological safety is the foundation of building a culture of collaboration, where diverse talents are cultivated and individual contribution thrives," he explains. "High-performing teams require a safe environment to collaborate, innovate, and excel. Without it, teams hesitate to share ideas and opinions, especially those that challenge the status quo."

At the executive level, effective collaboration creates a sense of unity among leaders, empowering them to make business decisions quickly, while also ensuring that the company adheres and abides by its core values. When this culture is at the core, the executive team can strategically address issues as a single, cohesive force. Ultimately, inclusive leadership becomes the fabric of a culture-centric leadership team and steers the organization toward its goals with unparalleled synergy.

Leaders who are uncomfortable with healthy tension might be tempted to avoid tough topics or impose their own ideas in order to "solve" a problem. But these interventions stop teamwork in its tracks. Instead, by acting as a facilitator and asking questions, inclusive leaders can create an environment where teams collaborate and solve issues together. That way, they are better able to learn and understand that the points that separate them are not as important as the singular goal that the team is trying to achieve together.

Highly effective business leaders also realize that collaboration doesn't stop with their own teams. Inclusive leaders also foster collaboration with their peers, across departments, with external partners, and beyond, as businesses and leaders are being asked to address wide-ranging societal challenges.

To build collaborative skills, it's imperative for leaders to foster open and transparent communication, creating an environment where everyone feels safe to express their ideas and opinions. To encourage the free-flowing exchange of ideas, inclusive leaders have to be comfortable taking a supporting role at times. Teams have a tendency to depend on the leader for answers, but leaders don't need to solve every problem. By asking strong questions and letting everyone else speak before they do, inclusive leaders give their teams the opportunity to arrive at the best solution themselves.

Inclusive leaders can cultivate high-performing teams at every level of their organizations by harnessing the power of collaboration. The following practices are among the ways collaborative leaders create high-performing teams:

Group Decision-Making: As a leader, it's imperative that your teams understand that success isn't tied to personal achievements alone, but in attaining collective goals and pursuing organizational outcomes. Inclusive leaders seek input from key stakeholders, whether they are peers or direct reports, to consider their ideas, needs, and perspectives when setting goals and milestones. Involving team members in the decision-making process leads to more effective outcomes and fosters a greater sense of community.

Diverse Perspectives: Innovative solutions happen when a variety of knowledge, viewpoints, and experiences come together. Leaders highlight the value that diverse perspectives bring to the creative process. They also strive to anticipate questions, concerns, and fears that team members may have. Creating space and opportunities for questions demonstrates a commitment to addressing issues and maintaining an environment where team members can contribute fully. For example, deep thinkers should be given enough time to process their thoughts and provide their opinions.

Effective Feedback: An inclusive leader uses feedback to identify the gap between behavior and success with the understanding that closing that space will lead to a stronger organization. It's essential that leaders approach feedback with a mindset of "we are going to do what is collectively right for the organization." Evaluations must center on "we"—what *we* want to achieve together, how *we*'ll tackle the challenge, and how *we*'ll work to improve together. Key to effective feedback is also being receptive to suggestions yourself, whether the feedback comes from a supervisor, peer, or team member.

Vulnerability: The essence of a good collaborator is asking for help when you need it. Publicly seeking assistance also encourages others to do the same. Being transparent about your need for help shows self-awareness and humility, which create the foundation for psychological safety and trust. By acknowledging another person's strengths and their importance to team efficiency, you also build their confidence and generate additional trust.

Authenticity and Healthy Conflict: An atmosphere of open and honest communication allows team members to feel safe expressing their thoughts and concerns without fear of judgment or repercussions. Candid discussions, where different viewpoints are heard and explored on the basis of their merits, should be encouraged. Remember, passion is welcome in any discussion, but personal attacks never are. By fostering an environment of psychological safety, team members can freely share ideas and contribute fully to collaborative efforts, ultimately leading to more effective and innovative outcomes.

Many Ways to Collaborate: Inclusive leaders understand that "collaboration" means different things to each person. Some people might initially be reluctant to give their opinions in a group setting, so it's important to give people different forums to collaborate. Establish procedures for your entire team to share their opinions, such as calling on each person at the end of a meeting. Some leaders find it helpful to ask each team member for feedback individually or request written responses. And remember, not every decision requires a meeting. Teams can also collaborate via email or instant messaging.

Highly effective business leaders know collaboration doesn't stop with their own teams. Inclusive leaders also foster collaboration with their peers, across departments, with external partners, and beyond, as businesses and leaders are being asked to address wide-ranging societal challenges.

CASE STUDY

Josh Haymond, Managing Partner of Vaco Raleigh, is an inclusive leader who works across the company with his peers from other locations in order to share trends and how the company is performing in different markets. He also schedules regular sessions with his Raleigh leadership team to ensure that each has an opportunity to share their observations and discuss concerns in a safe space.

That consistent feedback loop needs to happen; there needs to be scheduled time or else it doesn't get done effectively. We've taken time off of the floor consistently, so we can spend time together as a leadership group, so that we can be on the same page. If one of us is in vehement opposition to what someone else thinks, that's not going to result in a cohesive communication to our office. We want to make sure... the same message trickles down to everybody throughout the organization.

Statistics compiled by career platform Zippia speak to the issues that leaders like Vaco's Haymond and others face with building collaborative cultures, even among leadership teams. For example, the research team found:

- 86% of those in leadership positions cite "lack of collaboration" as the top reason for workplace failures
- 91% of employees rate their workplace as less than "very effective" for sharing and collaboration tools and systems
- Yet, 75% claim "teamwork and collaboration" in the workplace as "very important"

Statistics like these are a proofpoint demonstrating both the heightened importance of collaboration across organizations, as well as the gap between what leaders hope to build and what is actually happening. The hard work of creating inclusive leadership skills is one method for increasing collaborative practices, which holds the potential for redefining success for individual leaders and managers and the company as a whole. The payoff will be fueling nimble decision-making tailored for today's marketplace and the challenges that lay ahead.

SKILL-BUILDING AND EXERCISES

Often, leaders move into management roles because they are outstanding individual contributors, and many find it difficult to shift their focus from personal achievement to collective success. Yet, collaboration is essential for organizations and inclusive leaders because it unlocks competitive advantage. By growing this key capability, senior executives cultivate diverse teams, which then bolster the agile decision-making. By creating stronger collaboration, inclusive leaders build more successful teams, drive innovation, and lead their organizations to greater achievements.

Collaboration as a personal strength: As a collaborative leader, you can build a stronger team by serving as a role model for the skills you want to see, including building trusted relationships. The most productive teams—with the most engaged employees—are those where people know each other, support one another, and cheer each other on. One way you can help your team develop personal connections is to take a few minutes before every meeting to check in. Even in virtual meetings, you can spend a few minutes asking how everyone is doing and what is going on in their lives. More than idle chit-chat, these casual conversations generate feelings of belonging and contribute to team cohesion.

Collaboration as a personal area of opportunity: Building and maintaining trusted relationships is the foundation of sustainable collaboration. Identify colleagues you rely on and those who depend on you. Look for ways to help when you get nothing in return; offer a favor, support someone's agenda, or share ideas and resources. Approach every conversation with empathy and compassion to show that you care about other people's perspectives. Ask your colleagues for feedback, and let them know how you applied it. Colleagues who believe you genuinely need them are more likely to seek your help when they need it.

Collaboration as a team area of opportunity: Fostering a culture of collaboration is essential for success, but teamwork is impossible without psychological safety. Ideas flourish and innovation thrives when colleagues can share their honest input without fear of retaliation, criticism, or ridicule. Setting meeting agreements can promote psychological safety, especially among colleagues who don't know each other well. Standard expectations establish a framework of respect and mutual support that can grow into trust.

The following are a few common meeting agreements, but your team might feel comfortable setting their own protocols.

- Be fully present. Put down your phone, leave the email, and give your attention to your colleagues.
- Listen to understand. Absorb what your colleagues are saying instead of formulating your own response.
- Assume good intentions. When topics are contentious or passions run high, remind yourself that everyone is trying to reach the best solution possible. Don't take disagreements personally.

- Make space, take space. Give plenty of time for others in the meeting to express their opinions, and speak up if you have a concern.
- Take the lessons, leave the details. Respect the confidentiality of everyone in the meeting. Gossip and side conversations can kill trust within a team.
- Ask questions to gain clarity. If you don't understand something, it's your responsibility to ask questions until you do. Miscommunication and misunderstandings waste time and energy.

It's important to note that creating an inclusive, collaborative environment is a collective responsibility. When issues or conflict arise, take a moment to identify what the core issue is, then work to solve it *together*.

Remember, collaboration and psychological safety go hand-in-hand. High-performing teams require a safe environment to thrive, innovate, and excel. Without it, teams hesitate to share ideas and opinions, especially those that challenge the status quo.

Reflections

1. High-performing leaders can become focused on their own success, their own numbers, the output of their own team. However, true success happens only when leaders collaborate across departments and functions for the good of the entire organization. Think about a successful personal effort or a team project. Could you have saved time or money if you had partnered with another department? Can you duplicate your team's effort in another location or department by collaborating with another team?

_____

_____

_____

2. One of the barriers to collaboration is that leaders have prowess in their individual lines of business or areas of expertise. Consider how your team is structured, and then the company as a whole. Reflect how you can break down silos within your

organization by actively collaborating with leaders with different functions across a variety of departments. Jot down some immediate tactics you can take to increase collaboration with another leader important to your work. What are some long-term goals that will result in increased collaboration for you personally and your team?

6. CAPABILITY

Capability describes the proficient use of a leader's skills, knowledge, and behaviors to elevate team performance and achieve business outcomes. High levels of individual performance and functional excellence are a given for inclusive leaders. A capable leader is someone who naturally stands out, not only for their expertise, but for their ability to make everyone around them more productive, valued, and collaborative.

Capability instills confidence since employees are more likely to trust a leader who demonstrates subject matter expertise. A leader's expert guidance can ensure the success of a project, even when it has been delegated to a less-experienced team member. Employees can more easily get the resources they need when their boss has a deep understanding of the process and the objectives.

When leaders attain a C-suite role, the ability to perform at a high level is a given. Because there are bottom-line consequences when executives fail to meet their objectives, those on a leadership team have to be capable in their domain and expert in their subject matter. There is a critical shift in thinking that must occur, though. Truly exceptional leaders add value to the entire team, exponentially increasing their impact, not just in their own line of business.

"The most capable leaders have the emotional intelligence to inspire their team, develop meaningful relationships, and create psychological safety," explains Ferguson, TDM Co-founder and critically-acclaimed host of the "Diversity: Beyond the Checkbox" podcast. "They cultivate an inclusive workplace culture where everyone's unique talents are appreciated and all employees can perform without fear or worry about retribution."

But, she counsels, "Capability is not static. A leader must continually evolve with societal changes, client needs, and the ever-fluctuating economic landscape." For many people, navigating change and friction is difficult and often slows progress to a crawl. A capable leader will use their skills to eliminate barriers, thereby establishing a culture where teams come together to solve problems through better communications and collaboration.

Leaders who display capability are goal-oriented and look for ways to link team achievement to company objectives. Spending time with team members to educate them on how their respective responsibilities map to business outcomes creates clarity. This enables other members of the team to build capacity so that the leader can scale their own efforts.

This focus on the team is only half the battle. Capable leaders must hold themselves to the highest standards of excellence. They are accountable, and because they follow through, they prove their trustworthiness each day to team members, colleagues, and superiors. What we've seen in working with our own clients and in working with global executives is that high-performing leaders accept no excuses. They get things done!

Leaders who embody capability are committed to continuous improvement. They invest in lifelong learning, eagerly embrace feedback, and actively seek opportunities for enhancement. Ultimately, capability empowers leaders to exceed the expectations of their colleagues, teams, boards, and customers, driving both personal and organizational growth. The pivotal skills that allow capable leaders to foster a culture of excellence include effective delegation, problem-solving, teamwork, and meeting management.

Empower your team through strategic delegation: Savvy leaders use delegation to leverage individual strengths and ensure the entire team is aligned with overarching goals. Effective delegation ensures that the workload is distributed efficiently and fosters a sense of ownership and skill development among your employees. Successful delegation makes everyone on the team stronger.

Encourage better decision-making: Encourage brainstorming sessions, leverage diverse perspectives, and implement innovative solutions. This effort will demonstrate that you are a leader that is looking for the best ideas rather than seeking credit. The result will be sharper, faster problem-solving across the team and a more collaborative culture.

Support those around you: Regularly check in on progress, address concerns promptly, and create an environment where open communication flourishes. Your availability for collaboration sets the tone for a responsive and supportive leadership style. In turn, meet deadlines for items requiring your review and approval. Timely feedback is crucial to keep projects on track and prevent bottlenecks. Make sure that your team can progress smoothly by providing prompt review. Being mindful in this area demonstrates reliability, while also instilling confidence in your team's ability to execute.

Support team development and skill-building: Providing learning and development opportunities for your team is a key factor in retention. The more people learn, the more likely they are to be satisfied as part of the team. Slow down with team members to educate them in your areas of expertise and find outside resources when needed to develop new skills.

Lead effective meetings: Provide clear agendas, establish inclusive meeting protocols, encourage open dialogue, and actively involve everyone. Ask intentional questions to ensure full collaboration and inclusion. Fostering an environment where all voices are heard leads to a culture of belonging and results in enhanced innovation and problem-solving.

Celebrate achievements: Acknowledge and celebrate the achievements and capabilities of your team members. Recognizing someone's contributions demonstrates that you value them personally for their unique contributions, resulting in higher engagement, greater productivity, and enhanced team capability.

CASE STUDY

Joanne Lax is the inaugural recipient of the American Health Law Association's IDEA (inclusion, diversity, equity, accessibility) Champion Award. As an attorney who is visually impaired, she has been a trailblazer in championing inclusion. Her leadership and planning led to AHLA hosting a groundbreaking virtual Roundtable in May 2021. The Inclusion of People with Disabilities in the Delivery of Legal Services brought together decision-makers, diversity officers, and general counsel to discuss how to better serve disabled clients.

> As an attorney who is visually impaired, I felt first-hand the sting of being marginalized or dismissed several times during my career. A few potential clients categorically refused to hire me as a consequence of my disability—even though I tried hard to assure them that my firm and I had solid processes in place to ensure that their work would be done efficiently, effectively, and with the same quality as they should expect

from any of my sighted partners. Those experiences motivated me to educate the health law world about IDEA so that no one else with a disability would experience that kind of humiliation.

At the American Health Law Association, I served in many leadership positions that included IDEA responsibilities. That enabled me to help develop objectives, policies, procedures, and measurable goals that advanced IDEA throughout the association. By directly participating in AHLA IDEA programming for its membership, I was able to share actionable IDEA steps with health law professionals who could carry the message and the action steps back to their organizations for implementation. AHLA is both an example and a platform for the health law community to learn about, embrace, and implement successful IDEA initiatives.

I am proud of my role in helping AHLA understand the importance of including disability in the scope of IDEA. Too often it is an overlooked category. Many organizations focus exclusively upon the more core DEI groupings of race, ethnicity, religion, gender, and sexual orientation. AHLA embraced the broader definition, and even developed outward-facing programming to educate the health law community about it.

SKILL-BUILDING AND EXERCISES

Capable leaders understand that continuous improvement is necessary to meet the demands of a changing world. Highly effective leaders invest in lifelong learning, eagerly embrace feedback, and actively seek opportunities to enhance their professional expertise. Building capability is essential for leaders, but it takes more than a commitment to personal growth. Any efforts to improve must also include the drive to make your team better. By honing your capability as a leader, you will gain the knowledge and skills required to navigate challenges, cultivate innovation, and advance your team toward collective success.

Capability as a personal strength: Top leaders deftly navigate the countless immediate priorities that lead to business results, yet many are uncertain about the future. According to a 2024 PwC Global CEO Survey, 45% of respondents are "not confident that their companies would survive more than a decade on their current path." Strategic thinking can help you balance current performance with future opportunities.

Your ability to stay ahead of economic and operational disruptions and use them to your advantage will allow you to achieve personal success and give your organization a competitive advantage. Strategic adaptability enables you to anticipate possible risks before they escalate and pivot quickly when a crisis hits. The mindset also allows you to identify and seize emerging opportunities.

As a capable leader, you can foster a culture of agility and creativity by encouraging experimentation, learning from failures, and embracing continuous learning. Encourage your team to embrace new methodologies and technologies, such as Artificial Intelligence (AI) tools, to improve efficiency and solve problems faster. By cultivating adaptability, your team can respond quickly to changing circumstances without jeopardizing quality or performance.

Capability as a personal area of opportunity: Successful leaders regularly establish meaningful, achievable goals—for themselves and for their team. To elevate your capability, it's vital to set goals that align with corporate objectives and propel the team toward success. The following framework can help you do that:

1. Align your goals with the business's overarching mission.
2. Bring together a team of people whose skills, expertise, and perspectives complement each other.
3. Ensure adequate resources, and clearly define the roles and responsibilities of those on your team.
4. Explain why these objectives matter within the context of the company's mission and vision.
5. Keep goals aspirational, yet still achievable.
6. Track milestones, so you can tell whether the team is on track or needs to adjust.
7. Build personal relationships with members of the team that incorporate coaching, mentoring, and advising in areas of strength. This is often done informally outside of meetings. As the saying goes, "more is caught than taught," which requires proximity to team members.

Capability as a team area of opportunity: To more skillfully navigate today's business landscape, teams can become more effective and capable by staying aware of industry trends. Ongoing professional development should be part of every person's job description, whether the learning comes through books, articles, podcasts, courses, newsletters, or meeting with experts.

Individuals should be encouraged to share their insights with the team, so everyone can immediately apply the newfound knowledge. As a leader, you can also invest in tools and technology that boost team effectiveness. For example, generative AI platforms, like Chat GPT or Google Gemini, can be used as information-gathering resources or brainstorming partners to increase efficiency [see Appendix IV for more information about AI]. Gaining access to real-time data and analytics can also help the team develop the insights needed to respond to rapidly changing business environments.

Reflections

1. Many people become managers because of their expertise and knowledge, but sometimes the day-to-day demands of the job interfere with ongoing professional development. Capable leaders stay up-to-date with industry trends and acquire new abilities. Consider a professional skill that you would like to master or a certification that would complement your duties. Create a detailed plan to master the new skill, and include the resources you would need. What is a reasonable timeline or completion date? Can you enlist an accountability partner to keep you progressing in a timely fashion? Reflect on the favorable outcomes of your increased expertise, so you can remain enthusiastic about your progress.

2. Many leaders are strong individual performers, yet it is clear that winning organizations thrive based on team success. Consider a time when you might have performed well personally, but your team failed to meet expectations. Jot down some notes about how you could have collaborated more effectively? Were you reluctant to delegate responsibilities, because you could "do it better yourself"? Are there opportunities to mentor members of your team?

3. What would you think if another leader or your direct supervisor questioned your capability? If that were the case, how would you respond and what plan would you develop to increase this competency? Now, imagine you are having that same conversation with one of your direct reports? How does the discussion unfold and what are your expectations?

7. GROWTH MINDSET

Continuous growth is imperative for the success of executive teams and business outcomes; it allows leaders to leverage the thinking of diverse groups to drive innovation and evidence-based decision-making. By engaging in ongoing learning and discovery, organizations are able to stay on the pulse of customer needs and behaviors, while also fostering the development of their staff.

Leaders with a growth mindset are better prepared to successfully address challenges, capitalize on new opportunities, and drive continuous improvement. A leader's ability to make bold decisions, venture into uncharted territory, and embrace uncertainty is imperative for growth and innovation.

"There are many real-world business advantages in developing and strengthening a growth mindset, including the ability to leverage the diverse expertise within our teams and enhancing innovation," explains Rekha Daniel-Kimani, Regional Director, Head of Total Rewards, DEIB and Strategic HR Growth Operations at BAYADA Home Health Care, named among America's Greatest Workplaces for Diversity by *Newsweek* two years in a row.

"A growth mindset helps build a stronger culture and powers inclusive leadership, which enables the entire organization to become more resilient, adaptable, and focused on solving increasingly complex challenges," she says. "True growth as an inclusive leader lies in our ability to navigate uncharted territories, make confident decisions, and embrace uncertainty."

Inclusive leaders drive innovation and gather the data for better decision-making by leveraging the contributions of diverse groups. Make sure your team includes individuals with a variety of backgrounds, world views, and perspectives. You'll be a stronger leader if you surround yourself with people who inspire you and challenge you to grow—and then listen to and respect their input.

Being a growth-oriented leader means actively fostering a culture of teamwork, critical thinking, and inclusion. Often that means being the strongest facilitator in the room, not the person with the loudest voice. Inclusive leaders believe wholeheartedly that "the best idea wins," which spurs collaborative thinking.

Of course, leaders have strong opinions and ideas, but they also leave room for new information. You can drive toward your goals, yet still have humility and respect for other people's contributions. A leader with a growth mindset can be strong-willed, but not stubborn; self-assured and confident, but always open to new ideas.

A leader's professional growth must also include sharing knowledge with their team. This practice encourages collaborative education, while fostering an environment where everyone benefits from the collective insights garnered. Sharing knowledge helps teams connect, perform better, and become stronger as professionals. Additional advantages of knowledge sharing include saving money on training and capturing know-how, so that expertise doesn't escape your organization should an employee decide to leave the company.

Promoting a growth mindset will not only improve the efficiency and productivity of your team, but the attitude will also feed an inclusive workplace culture. According to the Harvard Business Review, employees who work at organizations that value and promote a growth mindset are 34% more likely to feel a strong sense of ownership and commitment to the company. These are the teammates most likely to help you create a stronger workplace culture and act as ambassadors for your company in the community.

Here are five actionable tips to help you promote continuous improvement, spark creative thinking, and encourage calculated business risks:

Encourage outside reading: Emerging leaders have an incentive to improve, so give your team articles or books that describe different ways of decision-making and problem-solving. One classic text is "Six Thinking Hats," by Edward de Bono, which explores how to investigate an idea or challenge from a number of perspectives and move beyond habitual ways of thinking.

Ask probing questions: One of the best ways to facilitate a growth mindset is by asking, "What's next?" The question will push your team out of their comfort zone, encouraging them to move beyond what they think they're capable of. Other questions to promote innovation are: "Is there a better way?" or "Is this the best use of our time?" or "How can we do this at lower cost?"

Establish a protocol for expansive thinking: As an inclusive leader, you can encourage the free exchange of ideas by making brainstorming a part of every meeting. There is immense value in using 10 or 15 minutes to explore radical thinking and progressive ideas. The regular habit of sharing out loud will spark innovation and curiosity, which lead to better business outcomes.

Reward risk-taking and recovery from failure: People might be reluctant to share suggestions or a new approach, because they don't trust their team or they aren't self-confident. To promote a growth mindset, there should be zero tolerance for retaliation, criticism, or ridicule. Make it clear that everyone is expected to contribute and every idea will be considered with respect. Encourage team members to propose new ideas, processes, and solutions, even if they entail some degree of risk.

Create a feedback culture: Make feedback a regular part of your team's process and use it as a tool to get the best results. Be sure to critique the idea and not the person. It's your responsibility to coach your team to see criticism as a learning opportunity. By creating a culture of ongoing dialogue—top-down, bottom-up, and peer-to-peer—you cultivate a growth mindset in your team.

A growth mindset demonstrates vulnerability, adaptability and resilience. Through sharing experiences, being transparent about mistakes, and recovering with confidence, an inclusive leader inspires their team to do the same, thereby creating a stronger leadership team across organizational roles and responsibilities. Maintaining tenacity in the face of risk and change empowers teams to confidently grow and innovate.

CASE STUDY

Erin Stone, Vice President of Samuel Lawrence Hospitality, a division of Hooker Furnishings, relies on a growth mindset and maintaining an attitude of curiosity to effect change across her organization. "I don't assume I know the answer," she says, "which opens me up to hear what's really being said, not just hearing what confirms my own thoughts and opinions." Her curiosity and openness to new ideas helped her identify several high-performing individuals who weren't on traditional management career paths.

> In my most recent role in residential furniture, I led our Relationship Management Operations team through a year-long restructuring, combining people from multiple

locations onto single teams and rethinking what functions those teams should cover. I was able to build a structure that played to the strengths of the individual contributors and build strong teams by getting curious about the people I managed.

As I talked to people about their own career trajectories and what type of work they were passionate about, I noticed that there were a few names that were frequently mentioned. These people were already performing at a higher level and were already leaders among their peers.

The result was that I was able to promote three women to leadership positions—two of whom were people of color. It's not enough to ask about experience and willingness to lead when you're looking for leaders. I had to get curious and find out who was a nascent leader and deserved an opportunity to grow that skill set.

SKILL-BUILDING AND EXERCISES

When we develop our capacity for learning, we set the tone for a growth-focused culture that expects and rewards continuous improvement. To inspire your team and others throughout your organization, share what you are learning, openly and often. These opportunities help create trust and communicate an expectation for continuous growth across the organization.

Growth Mindset as a personal strength: Your responsibility as a leader is to encourage others around you to expand their thinking, invest time and effort in continuous improvement, and embrace calculated business risks. Encourage your team to embrace challenges as learning experiences or "successful failures." When faced with difficult situations, emphasize the potential for growth and development that may result from the effort. Help team members develop resilience by emphasizing the importance of bouncing back from setbacks. Frame challenges as opportunities to build adaptability.

Growth Mindset as a personal area of opportunity: Leaders with a growth mindset actively seek opportunities to improve and eagerly embrace both compliments and criticism. Critical feedback can be especially valuable, because it alerts you to important changes you need to make. However, hearing negative comments isn't easy; it can make anyone upset or self-conscious. That's why it's important to prepare for tough conversations. Remind yourself that the critique is about your work—not you—and is designed to ensure success for the organization.

When someone gives you negative feedback, take a few moments to collect your thoughts instead of immediately becoming defensive. Ask for specific examples and suggestions, so you fully understand the criticism and their thought process. Finally, as with any feedback, thank the person for their comments. Remember, it takes courage to share difficult feedback, as tough words could damage your relationship. Thanking them opens the door to continued collaboration and learning.

Growth Mindset as a team area of opportunity: A key aspect of a growth mindset is taking risks and facing new challenges. And, the only way for individuals to innovate and grow is by stepping outside their comfort zone. Highly effective leaders can guide their colleagues through uncharted territory by focusing on the beneficial outcomes, recognizing the value of learning new skills, and reframing setbacks as growth opportunities. Leaders can also provide needed support, such as finding experts who can add valuable insights and setting aside time for professional development. Each stretch project will generate greater comfort with professional risks, and with each success, team members will learn to cooperate and communicate more effectively. As their achievements multiply, the team will build additional skills, become stronger collaborators, and expand their growth mindset.

Reflections

1. Think about the current challenges you're facing in your leadership role or those you anticipate encountering in the near future. Think about how you can approach these challenges with a growth mindset? Write down actions or strategies that you can take to turn these challenges into opportunities for growth.

_____

_____

_____

2. Many leaders—even with many years of success—have become risk averse, which hinders an authentic growth mindset. Were there times in the past when you took a risk and it didn't pay off. How did you deal with it? How did you communicate

with affected stakeholders and your supervisor and teammates? What did you learn from the experience, and how has it impacted your capacity for risk?

___

3. Identify individuals within your organization and industry who exhibit a thirst for knowledge, adaptability, and a forward-thinking mindset. Write down each person's strengths. How do their talents complement your own? How can you help them in return? Reach out to schedule time to meet, and be sure to communicate your reasons for the conversation. If the initial meeting goes well, make it a priority to connect regularly.

___

8. CULTURAL INTELLIGENCE

In the context of an increasingly globalized business landscape, cultural intelligence is an indispensable trait for executive teams striving to enhance their effectiveness and leadership capabilities. Leaders who show cultural intelligence build environments centered on belonging, empathy, and inclusion across diverse teams. They power inclusive leadership by establishing a shared commonality in understanding cultural cues, etiquette, and other culture-forward ideas.

Culturally intelligent leaders recognize that everyone has a different perspective, shaped by their cultural norms and traditions. By respecting everyone's unique worldview, inclusive leaders can cultivate welcoming workplaces where people feel valued and encouraged to contribute their best work. They also welcome new ideas and see each interaction as a learning opportunity. The resulting sense of belonging has many benefits, including a more collaborative workplace and a healthier focus on employee well-being.

The real-world outcomes of an inclusive culture are extensive, from higher retention rates and greater employee engagement to stronger innovation and faster decision-making. By empathetically responding to the human elements of business, culturally intelligent executives create opportunities for others to share difficult or uncomfortable information. They recognize that every person has unique talents and capabilities. This awareness enables them to navigate the complex dynamics of diverse teams with understanding, empathy and sensitivity.

Productive collaboration and next-level innovation are impossible without cultural intelligence, which enables inclusive leaders to build synergy within diverse groups. Any business that strives to remain relevant, agile, and competitive—regardless of location—will optimize its efforts by cultivating an inclusive workplace culture and leaders who are masters of cultural intelligence.

Lenovo is a global technology company specializing in designing, manufacturing, and marketing consumer electronics, personal computers, software, business solutions, and related services. The company has built on its success as the world's largest PC company by further expanding into growth areas that fuel the advancement of "New IT" technologies, including client, edge, cloud, network, and intelligence across server, storage, mobile, software, solutions, and services. Calvin J. Crosslin, Vice President/Chief Diversity Officer at Lenovo and President of the Lenovo Foundation, views cultural intelligence as a business advantage.

"By working to create a culture where your team acknowledges cultural differences, you can help your team forge meaningful relationships with colleagues and associates—no matter where they are from," Crosslin explains. "When you respect everyone's unique worldview, you can cultivate welcoming workplaces where people feel valued, included, and encouraged to contribute their best work."

Leaders with strong cultural intelligence know that just because someone else approaches a challenge differently, doesn't mean their tactics are better or worse. They also know how to recognize and honor cultural differences to create a strong team environment. That's not to say that cultivating cultural intelligence doesn't take effort. Even the most inclusive leader knows that being open to new opportunities and learning moments can help them be better managers and collaborators. Here are some practical strategies to enhance cultural intelligence:

Explore Underrepresented Voices and Diverse Perspectives: To expand your cultural intelligence, seek out voices and perspectives that you may not usually hear or consider. Read books, listen to podcasts, watch documentaries, and engage with resources that shed light on communities different from your own.

Uncover your Unconscious Bias: There are several ways that unconscious bias can forestall your curiosity about other cultures, therefore it's important to be aware of any assumptions you are making about people from different cultures. Humans naturally attribute qualities—both good and bad—to certain groups. However, when you know your biases, you can mitigate them by approaching every individual with curiosity and respect for their unique lived experience.

Foster Connections: Building relationships with people from diverse backgrounds is a powerful way to enhance cultural intelligence. Challenge yourself to connect with at least one new person every week. You will gain fresh perspectives, business leads, potential hires, and valuable learning opportunities through these connections.

Notice Body Language: Pay close attention to the nonverbal cues in your interactions. Body language can be universal in some aspects but can also vary significantly across cultures. Be flexible and adapt to the body language of those around you, mirroring their comfort levels.

Ask Clarifying Questions: Don't hesitate to ask questions when you are unsure about cultural norms. Observe and respectfully seek clarity. Questions like, "What is the usual tone of this meeting?" or "I noticed that . . . Can you tell me more about . . ." are excellent ways to bridge gaps in understanding. Don't assume that you are being understood or achieving your aims, just because you aren't receiving feedback. Different cultures have varied social etiquette when it comes to offering criticism or constructive feedback.

In essence, cultural intelligence equips executive teams with the tools to bridge cultural gaps; build strong, cohesive teams; and effectively navigate the complexities of a global business landscape. By nurturing cultural intelligence, executive teams can unlock their full potential as leaders and create workplaces that are inclusive, diverse, and collaborative.

CASE STUDY

Cultural intelligence equips executive teams with the tools to bridge cultural gaps; build strong, cohesive teams; and effectively navigate the complexities of a worldwide business landscape. Cultural intelligence helps leaders and organizations win in the global marketplace, explains **Shelley Willingham**, Chief Revenue Officer at The Diversity Movement.

> In the early 2000s, I had a marketing and sales consulting company, and one of my clients was John Deere, which manufactures agricultural and lawn care machinery. At the time, there was a huge influx of Spanish-speaking people settling in the community, and many of these new residents were launching landscaping businesses. I helped Deere craft a cross-cultural marketing campaign, so it could market more effectively to this growing entrepreneurial population.
>
> That experience highlighted an opportunity for me to help other companies connect with diverse populations. The company I founded, The National Organization

for Diversity in Sales and Marketing, focused on helping U.S. companies recognize the purchasing power of diverse populations and craft inclusive marketing strategies, free of stereotypes.

One of my clients was a travel company that refused to let same-sex couples come to their resorts. I asked the leadership team: "Do you know how much purchasing power and disposable income the LGBTQ+ community has?" Because the issue was framed as a business decision, the owners of the company were able to put their personal opinions aside and create a more welcoming environment at their properties.

Cultural intelligence is characterized by a willingness to form mutually beneficial relationships with individuals from a variety of backgrounds. My ability to engage with individuals who don't share my identity, perspective, or worldview has allowed me to navigate complex business relationships and provide value.

SKILL-BUILDING AND EXERCISES

Cultural mismatches of all sorts make communication difficult and get in the way of effective team collaboration, even if your team isn't geographically dispersed. By applying these practices and embracing the principles of cultural intelligence, senior business leaders can create a workplace where diversity is celebrated, unity is fostered, and innovation flourishes. Making the commitment to a culture of inclusion and understanding enables you to pave the way toward success in an increasingly diverse and interconnected world.

Cultural Intelligence as a personal strength: You can become an even stronger leader by helping grow the cultural intelligence of everyone on your team and across the organization. You can use your skills to help your colleagues communicate better, reduce misunderstandings, and build rich, rewarding interpersonal connections. Ensure your employees and coworkers feel that they can speak openly without embarrassment or retaliation. When there is psychological safety within a group and trust between teammates, everyone will bring new ideas and viewpoints to the group.

You can also establish cultural exploration as a part of everyone's professional development. Encourage your colleagues to approach unfamiliar situations with curiosity—ask questions and seek clarity when they are unsure. Invite them to research cultural practices and etiquette and share the newfound knowledge with the entire team. When meeting someone from a different culture, take time to understand their communication style and customs.

Cultural Intelligence as a personal area of opportunity: Culturally intelligent leaders recognize that biases shape everyone's perceptions and actions toward particular individuals or groups. Cultural intelligence hinges on an individual's capacity to set aside these preconceived assumptions, fostering inclusion and mutual respect. If left unchecked, unconscious bias can breed discrimination and unfairness. The first step toward cultural intelligence is to identify hidden biases. Several unconscious bias tools exist, and one of the most popular is Harvard's Implicit Association Test (IAT). While the process can be uncomfortable, it is not designed to evoke guilt or shame. When you understand and acknowledge any biases, you can then mitigate their influence on your actions and make better decisions.

Cultural Intelligence as a team area of opportunity: In team settings, it's vital to notice when cultural disconnects occur and deflect any cultural bias that can inhibit productive relationships. It's easy to take offense or make assumptions when someone acts in an unfamiliar way, but those assumptions are often wrong. Teams can improve their cultural awareness by practicing "generous assumptions," in other words, accepting that everyone means well and is doing their best. Instead of taking immediate offense, it's better to ask for clarity: "Can you explain what you meant by that comment?" Misunderstandings can often be resolved quickly with a clarification or apology. At the same time, the exchange provides an opportunity to learn about cultural differences.

Team leaders should also establish conflict resolution strategies to address situations that can't be immediately corrected. It's crucial to acknowledge cultural differences and establish protocols that promote comprehension and consideration among teammates. Leaders can encourage cross-cultural learning, as well as invest in tailored training that can help neutralize challenges and prevent misinterpretation. The result will be stronger relationships, which result in a harmonious and productive workplace environment.

Reflections

1. Leaders today must thrive in a global business community. The aim is to grow one's cultural intelligence, as well as among the members of your team. When you

consider your role and experiences, what steps can you take to increase your knowledge of other cultures, particularly their specific business practices?

2. Do you have a framework for managing the discomfort that comes with connecting across differences? What steps might you take to ease or eliminate that concern?

3. Cultural intelligence is a skill that flourishes with continuous learning and engagement with people from a variety of backgrounds. Make a list of your immediate circle of friends and trusted advisers, along with their cultural identity. Do they share similar backgrounds? Consider expanding your network by connecting with individuals who can offer a different lens. When was the last time you were in a situation when most of the people in the room did not share your identity?

9. RELIABILITY

In the pursuit of leadership excellence, the ability to consistently deliver results is paramount. A leader's reliability is the foundation for strong interpersonal relationships rooted in honesty and integrity. Inclusive leaders understand that trust is the currency of collaboration—reliability sustains it.

Being a reliable leader means following through on commitments, while also ensuring your actions are fair and accurate. The hallmarks of reliable leaders include dependability, dedication to high-quality work, and adhering to timelines and budgets. Every interaction is an opportunity to build trust and strengthen relationships—whether with colleagues, employees, or customers.

Reliability is essential in building high-trust cultures and high-performing businesses. According to research from the *Harvard Business Review*, trust is linked to a host of favorable outcomes.

Workers at high-trust companies report:

- 74% less stress
- 106% more energy at work
- 50% higher productivity
- 13% fewer sick days
- 76% more engagement
- 29% more satisfaction with their lives
- 40% less burnout than people at low-trust companies

Consulting firm Great Place to Work also ties increased levels of workplace trust to higher business performance and greater employee satisfaction.

Leaders who are reliable and consistent also act as standard bearers for the organization's mission and purpose. The alternative is a workplace driven by chasing the next shiny object or trying to hit constantly moving targets, which result in morale plummeting and projects rarely succeeding. Few people enjoy unpredictability or walking into work, wondering, "What kind of mood is the boss in today?" In business, as in life, uncertainty breeds confusion.

People perform better when they can follow a plan and know what is expected of them. Certainly these factors can change, based on new information or goals, but in the long run, a team guided by an inconsistent or unreliable leader is going to be stressed and anxious.

"Culture is fundamentally tied to reliability," says Jamie Ousterout, Chief Experience Officer at The Diversity Movement. "Trust can't be established if it's only senior male managers who express confidence, while front-line employees or women in leadership roles undergo a distinctly disparate experience. Consistency in the employee experience forms the bedrock of building a trustful and inclusive work environment."

Reliable leaders recognize that the trust of colleagues and employees hinges on the consistent excellence of their output and the timely communication of it. This trust, in turn, is foundational for creating psychological safety and fostering respect in the workplace.

Striving for reliability and dependability is much smarter than attempting to be perfect, which is unobtainable. By showing your team that you are consistent and setting clear expectations, everyone will understand how to get their job done in a productive way. To foster a culture of excellence, it's also vital to communicate transparently, prioritize collaboration, and maintain accountability as circumstances change. Working to build these important skills will elevate your leadership.

Set clear expectations: Establish clear and achievable expectations regarding goals, timelines, and deliverables. Ensure everyone understands their role and responsibilities. As a leader, delegate tasks and responsibilities effectively. Assign tasks to team members based on their strengths and expertise, and then trust them to deliver.

Communicate consistently and transparently: Maintain open and consistent communication with your team—transparency builds trust. Be proactive in sharing any challenges or delays, so your team can quickly adjust. Establish protocols for regular updates on projects—at 25%, 50%, and 75% completion—so you can offer collaborative, constructive feedback.

Greg Ng, Chief Executive Officer at consulting firm Brooks Bell, says consistency is often underrated as a leadership trait. Yet, consistency is what keeps organizations focused on their mission, and predictability enables teams to understand what is expected of them.

"Being a consistent leader means doing what you say you will do each and every time," Ng says. "As a leader, your predictable actions and confident decisions will guide your team and empower them to navigate challenges. Their collaboration will also increase and lead to enhanced creativity and problem-solving."

Prioritize collaboration and teamwork: Make sure your entire team knows that you expect them to work together to achieve the objective. Empower your team to ask for assistance as needed and offer assistance when appropriate. Seek ways to support them, while making it clear you have confidence in their abilities.

Face challenges with accountability: When unexpected circumstances arise, cultivate accountability by focusing on the stated objectives and then making prompt adjustments. When the pressure is intensifying, encourage your team and provide the support and resources they need. While it is not always easy, a reliable leader approaches setbacks as opportunities for learning and improvement, while also working with the team to identify strategies to prevent them in the future.

Reliability is foundational and can always be enhanced. By focusing on improving your feedback, communication, and accountability, you'll continue to cultivate this crucial skill while also fostering a culture of consistent achievement and growth.

CASE STUDY

Reliable leaders exhibit unwavering determination regardless of challenges. They are resilient and persistent, while demonstrating the fortitude to persevere when confronted with obstacles. As an immigrant, **Edessa Polzin**, the Manager of Learning Partnerships at the American Marketing Association (AMA), has had to navigate significant challenges to achieve success in the United States. Her experiences have taught her the value of what she calls "grit."

> As an immigrant and a person of color, I've encountered my fair share of hurdles. While my immigration journey to the United States was a complex, time-consuming process filled with paperwork, interviews, and financial strains, my determination was my driving force. It helped me push through the maze of regulations and setbacks, always believing that overcoming each obstacle was getting me a step closer to my goal.
>
> This trait has extended into my professional life, where I've navigated uncertainties and obstacles as a marketer, including my role as a chapter leader at the AMA. It's what propels my efforts to make a meaningful impact and advocate for diversity, equity, and inclusion.
>
> I've learned that success often demands resilience, adaptability, and an unwavering commitment to one's goals. It's not about being the smartest or most talented; it's about having the determination to persevere, learn, and grow. So, grit, exemplified in moments like my immigration journey, has allowed me to thrive and inspire others to do the same.
>
> However, it's also vital to pair grit with genuine empathy.
>
> Resilience and a steadfast commitment to your goals are crucial for personal and professional success, so be ready to overcome barriers and challenge the norm. But remember that being an inclusive leader isn't just about your personal journey; it's about fostering an environment where everyone's experiences are valued. This is where genuine empathy comes in. Actively listen, understand diverse perspectives, and amplify the voices around you. To be an inclusive leader means leading with determination and ensuring that everyone, regardless of their background, feels valued and empowered.

SKILL-BUILDING AND EXERCISES

As leaders, reliability means much more than finishing to-do lists or doing a good job. Reliable leaders are catalysts for overall excellence, building stronger teams within an environment of trust and accountability. When teams are filled with people who prioritize reliability, the entire organization wins.

Reliability as a personal strength: Highly reliable leaders can sometimes become so focused on their professional goals and responsibilities that they ignore their own personal well-being and risk burnout. While certain situations may demand increased work hours, perpetual 80-hour workweeks signal a potential problem. When job demands are high, reliable leaders need a strategic roadmap—one that ensures consistent results, yet safeguards against exhaustion.

Effective tactics include setting priorities, delegating responsibilities, growing efficiency with continuous learning, and optimizing the capabilities of their team. As you create your personal plan of action, consider which strategies will best suit your needs, and don't forget to prioritize self-care. By investing in your physical and mental health, you can role model the advantages of an equitable work-life blend and demonstrate the importance of resilience to your entire team.

Reliability as a personal area of opportunity: It's important to note that being a reliable, dependable leader doesn't mean that you have to take on every project. In a high-stakes professional environment there can be enormous pressure to say "yes." Agreeing to too many initiatives, though, can actually sabotage a leader's overall reliability, while also undermining their team's effectiveness.

New leaders might assume that saying "no" will harm professional relationships. Yet, many senior executives would counter that learning this skill is an important managerial trait. In fact, colleagues and other stakeholders will respect individuals who thoughtfully consider the details around how new projects and initiatives can be successfully completed. Reliable leaders thoughtfully weigh different options, and carefully choose where to invest energy and effort. By establishing boundaries, a leader shows they value integrity, transparency, and exceptional results.

Reliability as a team area of opportunity: The familiar adage is that "teams are only as strong as their weakest link." Each person has a role, and how they perform has a direct impact on whether any given project will succeed or fail. Strong teams operate within an environment of trust and accountability, neither of which is possible without authentic and transparent communication. The leader has a responsibility to communicate their objectives, but team members also have a duty to alert the group to potential pitfalls, delays, or other obstacles. Reliable team members also communicate a willingness to help if their workload is light and ask for assistance if they feel overwhelmed. When the entire team is comfortable sharing insights and challenges alike, then problem-solving becomes a shared endeavor, and teams combine efforts to find innovative solutions.

Reflections

1. In your journey to become an even more reliable leader, it's essential to reflect on your current practices and strategies for holding both yourself and your team accountable. Think about recent instances when someone on your team failed to meet expectations. How did you respond to these situations? Did your feedback inadvertently discourage or demotivate the individuals involved? Were your comments clear, constructive, and forward-focused? List some ways you can give more valuable, actionable feedback.

___

___

___

___

2. When delegating assignments to your team, how are you working to ensure they complete the task? Do you share overall objectives and let them decide the most effective process? Or do you detail exactly how you want something done? List some ways you can encourage your team to solve problems and collaborate to achieve organizational goals.

___

___

___

___

3. By taking the time to establish a framework for success, you can increase your team's reliability, while fostering a culture of growth and attention to quality. Do you provide space for regular check-ins to monitor progress and provide needed support?

Write down some ideas for building the necessary framework and how you might present it to your direct reports.

10. SELF-AWARENESS

Leaders who possess self-awareness are constantly attuned to the impact of their words and actions on others, allowing them to adapt and lead with greater efficacy. Self-aware leaders are acutely conscious of their thoughts, language, behaviors, and biases. As a result, they are able to make more informed decisions, build trusting teams, and address the subtle influence of hidden biases on both personal interactions and the broader organization.

A key benefit of self-awareness is a deep understanding of one's strengths and gaps. Self-aware leaders harness the power of a supportive network, including family, friends, mentors, colleagues, and coaches. This network provides valuable guidance, development opportunities, and emotional support, allowing leaders to progress while understanding the outcomes of their actions.

"Leaders who embrace self-awareness foster an environment centered on authenticity, empathy, and adaptability. Inclusive leaders leverage their support network to educate themselves on their biases and how they impact their decisions and behaviors," explains Danielle Pavliv, Chief Diversity & Inclusion Officer at SAS, a multinational software developer.

It's not surprising that self-awareness is the strongest predictor of overall success for leaders, according to a study published in the *Harvard Business Review*, accounting for 30% of the variation in leadership effectiveness. People who see themselves with clarity and understand their impact on others are better leaders and even happier human beings, as well.

However, achieving and maintaining self-awareness can be challenging, and it gets harder as executives advance professionally. According to the *HBR* report, many leaders claim to have self-awareness, but only a small fraction of people—around 10 to 15 percent—actually embody this trait.

Experience can make leaders less apt to question their assumptions, less open to conflicting points of view, and more likely to rely on their existing knowledge. As leaders gain personal power, they are also more likely to become overconfident in their own abilities. To nurture self-awareness, executive leaders must commit to continuous learning through self-reflection, regular feedback from trusted advisers, and objective assessments.

"Ongoing evaluation is critical in growing as a leader, particularly as we build self-awareness, a key skill in making well-informed decisions, developing cohesive teams and addressing the influence of hidden biases," explains Ferguson, who led the team that created TDM LeaderView.

To foster a culture of excellence, it's vital to create safe spaces for free-flowing dialogue, consider other perspectives, understand other people's priorities, and give and receive feedback. These pivotal skills will elevate your inclusive leadership skills and set an inspiring example for others to follow.

Consider perspectives other than your own: Cultivate empathy by considering reasons why someone might have a different perspective than you. Challenge yourself to empathize with their viewpoint and understand the underlying motivations or experiences that shape their perspective. Learning about other cultures and other worldviews also helps self-aware leaders meet the demands of a rapidly changing and increasingly global business landscape.

Promote safe spaces for open dialogue: Create an environment where free-flowing discussion is encouraged, and team members feel safe sharing their perspectives and concerns. Actively listen to their feedback, demonstrate your willingness to consider their viewpoints, and foster a culture of mutual respect and inclusivity.

Understand other people's needs and motivations: Practice heightened awareness of the needs, wants, and motivations of others. Pay attention to cues that might not be immediately obvious, such as their level of engagement, anxiety, or confidence. This awareness allows you to tailor your interactions and support to better meet their individual needs. Develop the habit of holding back your immediate response when interacting with others. Instead, take a moment to consider various responses and their potential consequences. This pause allows you to demonstrate an awareness of the needs and feelings of others, leading to more thoughtful and constructive interactions.

Ask for frequent evaluations and regular feedback: No one can achieve their full potential if they don't know what's working, what's not, and what to do differently. Self-aware individuals actively seek opportunities to improve and eagerly embrace both compliments and criticism. Inclusive leaders harness the power of a supportive network, including family, friends, mentors, colleagues, and coaches. This network provides valuable guidance, development opportunities, and emotional support. Honest critiques from these trusted advisers will allow you to monitor your performance and understand how your behavior is interpreted by others.

Executives who see themselves with clarity and understand their impact on others have the power to supercharge their own performance as well as that of their team. As a foundational inclusive leadership capability, self-awareness sets the stage for continuous growth, meaningful collaboration, and highly productive, empathetic relationships. By actively seeking a variety of perspectives, creating psychologically safe workplaces, understanding others' needs and motivations, and cultivating a culture of feedback, you can become a more inclusive, effective leader and propel your organization toward lasting success.

CASE STUDY

Self-awareness is a key trait for inclusive leaders, allowing them to leverage diversity, equity, and inclusion (DEI) best practices to create psychologically safe environments where creativity and innovation can flourish. **Bridgett "BT" Tabor,** the Diversity, Equity and Inclusion Senior Manager at BAYADA Home Health Care, is responsible for executing DEI initiatives and leading cross-functional working groups that promote employee engagement and retention. As someone who is constantly challenging herself to achieve personal and professional excellence, Tabor has a clear-eyed view of her strengths, challenges, and influences.

> Self-awareness has been an invaluable asset in my DEI journey. It has significantly enhanced my decision-making abilities and provided me with a broader perspective.

While it can be tempting to approach situations with biases based on my own diversity identifiers, I consistently strive to avoid such tendencies. I believe in considering multiple angles and understanding the potential impacts on the business or the group I am advocating for. Self-awareness allows me to see beyond immediate concerns and take a more holistic approach to creating long-lasting change.

Being self-aware means recognizing my own weaknesses or areas where I may lack knowledge. This awareness enables me to confidently seek assistance from others who possess the expertise and information I need to make informed decisions. I understand the importance of collaborating with a diverse range of voices and perspectives to ensure that my decisions are well-rounded and considerate of all stakeholders. By embracing self-awareness, I can drive strategic initiatives that not only address the present challenges but also lay the foundation for the future.

SKILL-BUILDING AND EXERCISES

Executives who embrace self-awareness lead with authenticity, empathy, and adaptability. They nurture an environment where teams operate at peak efficiency and work collaboratively, thereby fostering personal and organizational growth.

Self-Awareness as a personal strength: As a self-aware leader, you already know that a culture of frequent feedback sets the stage for better collaboration and consistent professional growth. Feedback is also one of the best ways to foster self-awareness within your team and throughout the workplace. However, if your organization doesn't have a culture of frequent feedback, you can acclimate your colleagues to the process by asking, "May I offer you some feedback?"

On the surface, you are offering the listener an opportunity to learn and become more self-aware. However, by first asking if the person is ready for feedback, instead of launching immediately into your comments, you give them time to prepare, setting the stage for more receptive listening. Throughout your conversation, notice how the other person is responding. Watch their body language, so you can tell if they are becoming uncomfortable or confused.

By noticing how your comments are received, you can respond with empathy—pausing the conversation or asking if the other person has questions. The respectful exchange will increase mutual trust by showing that you care about the other person and want to help them learn and grow.

Self-Awareness as a personal area of opportunity: Self-awareness has significant benefits, leading to more connected, empathetic, and powerful leadership. Self-aware leaders are committed to ongoing self-reflection, willing to embrace vulnerability, and dedicated to understanding the intricacies of team dynamics. In order to enhance your self-awareness, consider these tactics.

- **Understand how to best use your strengths:** Self-awareness entails evaluating your influence in each situation to ensure you are working toward your goals and the goals of the organization.
- **Look for patterns:** Think about your leadership tactics that typically lead to positive results. Embrace what works best and strive for those outcomes. Continue to fine-tune those traits and methods for greater impact.
- **Embrace self-evaluation:** Continual reflection of various decisions and their outcomes fosters awareness. Take time to reflect before, during, and after interactions, both positive and negative. Ask yourself: Why did things go the way they did? What was your impact on the outcome? And how could you approach things differently in the future to create better or faster results?

Self-Awareness as a team area of opportunity: Self-awareness profoundly influences team dynamics and organizational success. Leaders who embrace self-awareness foster an environment centered on authenticity, empathy, and adaptability. To build self-awareness within their team, leaders can promote the "PAUSE method"—a strategic approach that allows individuals to navigate their biases by pausing and reassessing before making judgments or statements that could perpetuate bias.

PAUSE is an acronym representing five steps:

1. **P**ay attention to what's happening
2. **A**cknowledge your reactions, judgments, and interpretations of the situation
3. **U**nderstand what other reactions, judgments, and interpretations might be possible

4. **S**earch for productive solutions,
5. **E**xecute intentional plans.

The PAUSE method is about consciously taking stock of your internal reactions and judgments, acknowledging their existence, understanding alternative perspectives, and searching for the most constructive approach before acting. By adopting this method as a best practice, team members can become more self-aware individually and tap that understanding to help the group become more cohesive.

Reflections

1. Reflect on a recent project, campaign, or implementation. List how you encouraged honest and constructive feedback from your peers and other stakeholders. Write down some thoughts about how you might better encourage feedback with your teammates and reports. These discussions will help create a workplace where individuals understand themselves better, embrace personal growth, and become more effective leaders, ultimately fostering a culture of empathy, growth, and innovation.

_____

_____

_____

_____

2. Consider how your key personality traits (such as risk-tolerance or adaptability) influence your judgment. Think about a proposal or business opportunity that you decided not to pursue. Were you reluctant to move forward because you believed it was the wrong decision for the company or because you don't like change?

_____

_____

_____

_____

3. Think about an initiative that you decided to act on, yet it didn't achieve the results you had hoped. Were you eager to pursue the new project because it was personally fascinating? Did you have all the data you needed to make the right decision? Was the rest of your executive team excited about the project or were there dissenting opinions and differing viewpoints? Being able to answer critical questions like these enables leaders to weigh options based on facts—not emotions—and ultimately make the best decisions for their organization.

The Future of Inclusive Leadership

11. INCLUSIVE LEADERSHIP ON A GLOBAL STAGE

Leaders who embed inclusive practices into their foundational skill set create a ripple effect. Their teams, buoyed by a sense of belonging and trust, become engaged, innovative, and high-performing. As these teams flourish, the entire operation thrives. An organization fueled by inclusive leadership experiences reduced turnover, amplified creativity, and enhanced collaboration. These elements collectively elevate bottom-line results, both for short-term benefit and toward future success.

There are competing forces actually pulling people apart, including the isolating factors from hybrid and remote workplaces and how texting and direct messaging platforms have replaced telephone calls and face-to-face meetings. For corporations with far-flung global operations, the foundational principles of inclusive leadership can help overcome these challenges. Actively putting culture at the forefront allows people to form meaningful relationships with colleagues and associates—whether they work remotely, in a hybrid environment, or with coworkers on the other side of the world.

Allegro MicroSystems, headquartered in Manchester, New Hampshire, is a global semiconductor leader in sensor and power integrated circuits and photonics. The technology company has design and applications centers located across the Americas, Europe, and Asia, and a manufacturing facility in the Philippines. Julie Rousseau, Director of People Management, puts inclusive leadership first via a rather straightforward directive; she deliberately takes time to learn about other cultures. Rousseau recognizes that the commitment enables leaders to strengthen their engagement with teams regardless of location or nationality.

"Allegro is globally dispersed in several countries, and cultural awareness can be a challenge," Rousseau explains. "Respecting others and being patient are two really important qualities. Empathy plays a big part; listening skills are very important. DEI really comes down to treating people like human beings, treating people with respect, and understanding that not every human is like me."

Alan King oversees Workplace Options as it delivers high-quality care (digitally and in-person) to 80 million people in more than 200 countries and territories. Inclusive leadership takes on new meaning when a global crisis erupts, like the ongoing war in Ukraine. WPO had to respond fast as the war broke out, King explains:

> We were able to mobilize quickly and provide critical support to those in need, despite the challenges of a rapidly evolving reality on the ground, the destruction of communication and delivery infrastructure, and the sudden migration of millions of refugees. This experience, coupled with that of the pandemic, reinforced the necessity and value of our work in a world characterized by continuous volatility and change.

What we see in the experiences of leaders like King and Rousseau is a commitment to the profound potential of culture-centric values on building and strengthening organizational resilience. Whether it is helping a front-line worker in Asia or Arkansas understand how their work ties to a global organization's strategies or finding mental health resources for a family experiencing the trauma of warfare, an inclusive leadership mindset enables executives to move fast and place people (customers, employees, vendors, suppliers, and more) at the center of their thinking.

As the world constantly grows more interconnected, inclusive leadership transcends borders, growing a workplace that thrives on varied perspectives and lived experiences internally and then pushes these ideas out to external stakeholders. These executives understand that inclusivity and belonging are strategic imperatives for navigating the complexities of diverse global markets and cultures. By embracing inclusive leadership, executives forge robust connections, stimulate innovation, and fortify their organizations for whatever change may lie just beyond the horizon.

BUILDING DIVERSE TEAMS: TAPPING INTO THE POWER OF DIFFERENCES

Lucky organizations employ great leaders, but strategic organizations train their leaders to be great. The most important lesson for any leader—especially if they have been an outstanding individual contributor—is to shift their focus from their own accomplishments to their team's performance. Effective leaders have to direct the work, not do the work.

If leaders struggle because it's not about them anymore, they will have a difficult time becoming a good leader. New managers who don't put the team first might hold onto high-profile assignments, make decisions without getting team input, take personal credit for others' work or ideas, or blame their direct reports for any failures. These behaviors destroy team cohesion, undermine trust, and sabotage productivity.

People-leaders should be encouraged to build relationships with their direct reports through weekly one-on-one meetings. By getting to know their colleagues, leaders can play to team strengths and shore up individual weaknesses. Small everyday actions and interactions can demonstrate that a leader is trustworthy and inclusive. Likewise, small acts of exclusion or favoritism can undermine trust and have lasting negative consequences.

"As a leader, interpersonal skills are critical. Listening, communication, negotiation, public speaking—all of those things are super important if you're going to lead people. You cannot hide behind your phone or keyboard. You have to be approachable, and you have to be open to both criticism and commentary," says Jim Sills, president and CEO of M&F Bank, the second-oldest African American financial institution in the United States.

For senior leaders guiding global organizations, the focus on diverse teams can be a catalyst for innovation, adaptability, and enhanced problem-solving, which has taken on new significance as more organizations are staffed by hybrid knowledge-workers from different backgrounds and demographic groups. The value of a fully engaged team is its varied experiences and perspectives.

An example of global inclusive leadership is Microsoft, where CEO Satya Nadella championed diversity within teams, which has led to new products and services that resonate with a worldwide customer base. Nadella has been a catalyst for leading Microsoft's view of an interconnected marketplace and created teams that better understand and address the diverse needs of customers, no matter where they are headquartered. The Microsoft leadership team also recognizes that the organization should be a role model for other corporations.

"We are a global company and have a responsibility that the folks who work at Microsoft mirror everyone," says Lauren Gardner, Vice President of Global Talent Acquisition. "There should be equal opportunity for success. Companies have a significant responsibility to democratize."

As challenges become more complex and multifaceted, leaders who have focused on inclusivity have an edge in developing comprehensive solutions. A diverse team naturally addresses problems from various angles, drawing on a wealth of experiences and insights. Companies like Microsoft, guided by leaders who understand the intrinsic value of diversity, exemplify how embracing differences is a business imperative that positions organizations at the forefront of global success.

AUTHENTIC LEADERSHIP: ALIGNING VALUES WITH ACTIONS

Collaborative leaders understand that a unified team is key to effective decision-making and upholding an organization's core values. By bringing leaders together as a single, cohesive force, these leaders steer the organization toward its goals with unparalleled synergy.

Here are some actionable tips for harnessing the power of collaboration and creating stronger, more effective teams:

1. **Promote Inclusive Decision-Making:** Continue to include your team in decisions whenever appropriate and possible. Inclusive decision-making results in more effective outcomes and fosters a stronger sense of community and ownership among team members.

2. **Embrace Diverse Perspectives:** Encourage individuals to collaborate by recognizing the value of combining different knowledge and experiences to find innovative solutions to problems. Highlight that diverse perspectives can lead to novel and effective solutions. Strive to anticipate questions, concerns, and fears that team members may have during the collaboration process. Create space and opportunities for questions, demonstrating your commitment to addressing these issues and maintaining an environment where team members can contribute fully. For example, give time for deep thinkers on your team to process their thoughts and provide their opinions.

3. **Model Vulnerability:** The essence of a good collaborator is asking for help when you need it, and publicly seeking assistance encourages others to do the same. Admitting that you need help shows self-awareness and vulnerability, which create the foundation for psychological safety and trust. By acknowledging another person's strengths and their importance to team efficiency, you also build their confidence and generate more trust.

4. **Foster Honest Communication and Healthy Conflict:** Create an atmosphere of open and honest communication where team members feel safe expressing their thoughts, concerns, and feedback without fear of judgment or repercussions. Encourage candid discussions where different viewpoints are heard and explored on the basis of their merits. Emphasize that passion is welcome, but personal attacks are not. By fostering this environment of psychological safety, you enable team members to freely share ideas and contribute fully to collaborative efforts, ultimately leading to more effective and innovative outcomes.

Collaboration is essential because it unlocks competitive advantage. By embracing the power of collaboration and actively fostering a culture of inclusivity and teamwork, senior business leaders can build stronger, more successful teams, drive innovation, and lead their organizations to greater heights.

Together, as unified, diverse teams, we can shape the future of our organizations and make a lasting impact on the business world.

ESG, SUSTAINABILITY, AND INCLUSIVE LEADERSHIP

An environmental, social, and governance (ESG) perspective is more than a worldview. ESG is a performance indicator that organizations across the globe are using to measure information about corporate behavior in these three critical categories. Actually, ESG as a mental map has developed into a methodology for socially conscious consumers and investors to align their financial decisions with their personal values.

ESG metrics enable companies to measure, track, and report their ethical impact and environmental sustainability. Critics of ESG—including many lawmakers from oil- and gas-producing states—dislike ESG because of its emphasis on promoting social goals like lowering carbon emissions rather than maximizing shareholder returns regardless of the consequences for the planet or humankind.

However, reporting ESG does more than signal that a company is a good corporate citizen. Investors have flocked to companies with high ESG scores because they are more profitable, more sustainable, and better able to manage risk. Companies with high ESG scores are also more likely to be diverse, culture-centric organizations, because diversity, equity, and inclusion practices strengthen and enhance all three elements of ESG. As consumers, shareholders, and investors become increasingly values-oriented, corporate leaders can't afford to ignore the double benefits of DEI and ESG.

From this perspective, the tie between ESG and inclusive leadership is clear. One influences the other as companies and leaders push to create a business environment that does less harm, while still meeting organizational objectives. Indeed, the Securities and Exchange Commission (SEC) and other global regulatory agencies are increasing pressure for companies to disclose information such as board diversity, hiring practices, and pay equity.

Organizations that measure their DEI performance—and include that information in their ESG reporting—are better able to objectively demonstrate their commitment to ethical business practices. By linking DEI and ESG, culture-centric companies can improve their brand reputation, connect with customers, and attract more investors.

ESG Metrics and Inclusive Leadership

For the time being, organizations have leeway in measuring ESG metrics based on individual preferences and commitments. Each major category of ESG criteria—environmental, social, and governance—covers a wide range of issues that have historically been excluded from investment and purchasing decisions. Common metrics include:

- **Environment**—These metrics focus on a company's environmental impact and include greenhouse gas emissions, pollution, water use, and natural resource depletion.
- **Social**—These metrics reflect the way a company engages with its employees and how it influences the well-being of the community. This pillar considers metrics around diversity, employee satisfaction, safety incidents, volunteerism, and taxes.
- **Governance**—These metrics test a company's commitment to purpose and accountability. Included in this analysis is a standard to measure ethical behavior and risk. Governance factors include board diversity, succession planning, and executive compensation.

Inclusive leadership—and other people-focused strategies like DEI—should be the foundation for an organization's ESG strategy, because programs that boost employee engagement also increase collaboration, productivity, and innovation, leading to a company's sustainability and success.

For example, the impact of Employee Resource Groups (ERGs), a common component of DEI infrastructure, can be measured, tracked, and included in social metrics. One study found that 50% of ERG members reported increased job satisfaction and an intent to remain at their job long-term, helping employers lower recruiting costs.

Companies that make an authentic commitment to ERGs are finding innovative methods for cultivating and developing their future leaders. Cisco, for example, has 28 ERGs with more than 30,000 employees around the globe taking part. The value for the company, ERG membership boosts employee engagement, enabling them to "network, develop leadership skills, serve as change agents, and learn to be informed allies to various cultures and perspectives."

Board diversity, a frequently reported governance metric, is another powerful indicator of success. Boards with multi-dimensional diversity have been shown to be better equipped to guide their companies through tough times, leading to increased profitability, greater innovation, and lower risk. According to a report published in *Inc.* magazine, companies with diverse boards were better prepared to survive and thrive during the Covid-19 pandemic.

In Europe and the United Kingdom, the focus on women in leadership, particularly in the C-suite and boards of directors, has revealed a direct correlation between gender diversity and profitability. For example, the International Monetary Fund (IMF) looked at 2 million organizations across 34 European countries and found that companies with more women in top leadership were more profitable.

In "Women Count 2022," authors Margaret McDonagh and Lorna Fitzsimons, Co-Founders of The Pipeline, boldly declare, "To continue to systematically exclude women from Executive Committees and the most senior roles in top firms is an act of unbelievable folly." Their study showed that simply moving to a "balanced" executive leadership team across the UK Financial Times Stock Exchange (FTSE) 350 could increase national GDP by 2.5%. "Each year," they explain, "the UK is losing the equivalent of more than the defense budget, the entire schools budget, and triple the police budget, because of gender imbalance at the top of our companies."

Organizations with a strong ESG focus also tend to be financially successful overall. For instance, software company Salesforce is an ESG industry leader. The company has already achieved net-zero operational carbon emissions and has even bolder sustainability goals established for the future. In addition, they've allocated $16 million toward equal pay initiatives and established a racial equality and justice task force.

What we see in our own clients and at organizations globally is that a sustained commitment to inclusive leadership and the tenets of ESG combine to create a powerful strategy for long-term success. As competition heats up to attract socially responsible investors, consumers, and employees, these two intertwined strategies will only grow in importance.

Even if an organization has yet to launch a full-scale ESG program, inclusive leaders can use its principles to improve their companies. For example, a regional company could center relationships with its employees and the community, leading to a concerted effort to reduce its carbon footprint or partner with local suppliers.

Inclusive leadership as a core element of an executive's management ethos strengthens the tie between employees and their communities.

EXERCISES

There may be no more difficult task than to lead a global team or organization. The challenges exceed what most leaders take for granted, including language barriers, technology disconnects, cultural norms, and time differences. Yet, global business is the future of leadership. This profound shift necessitates a fundamental reevaluation of executive strategies.

While the principles of inclusive leadership will transform all leaders, they might be even more critical for a global leader or leadership team. These executives are facing added challenges each day, which makes a focus on culture-centric leadership more essential. Success is no longer defined solely by performance metrics, but has expanded to include ideas that cut across barriers, from trust and innovation to resiliency and enhanced collaboration. Culture is the cornerstone for organizations operating on a global stage.

Reflections

1. Consider a scenario where you and your team must consider perspectives from employees and stakeholders across diverse locations. What strategies would you use to ensure everyone's voice is heard?

_____

_____

_____

2. Reflect on your interactions with colleagues from diverse cultural backgrounds. What cultural nuances did you notice? How did these impact communication and collaboration? Were your interactions different for senior leaders than for direct reports?

3. Imagine you are preparing for an overseas trip. What steps might you take to prepare for the trip and meetings with leaders from different backgrounds?

4. When you think about ESG and its growing influence globally, how does it affect your leadership team and organization? If your company tracks ESG metrics, what could be done better or more frequently to talk about accomplishments? If you are not using an ESG framework, how might your organization use its principles?

12. WHY INCLUSIVE LEADERSHIP MATTERS

In a world marked by evolving workplace dynamics and fueled by innovation, the call to embrace inclusive leadership echoes loud and clear. Executives at every level, from the C-suite to frontline managers, must recognize that inclusivity is a strategic imperative.

By weaving inclusive practices into their leadership skill set at the most fundamental level, leaders amplify the impact of their teams, foster trust, and ignite unity. As leaders take up this mantle, organizations become incubators of innovation, collaboration, and sustainable success.

The primary focus centers on the creation of a thriving culture, a leadership aim whether the team is in San Francisco or Singapore. In most instances, this transformation must begin at the C-suite or board level. "The executive team has to visibly support the defining, shaping, and communication about the culture and why it matters to the company," a report by global consultancy Heidrick & Struggles explained. "The executive team and the board give credibility to the importance of the issue through their visible support and attention."

Ownership at the top of the organization signals to the whole team that the issue is important, one that cuts across the day-to-day challenges all leaders and organizations face. "In this way," the report outlined, "companies can keep culture from falling to the wayside when it is not a burning issue. It has to be owned by the board and the executive team."

STRATEGIES FOR A MORE INCLUSIVE FUTURE: SUSTAINABILITY AND CONTINUAL GROWTH

Attracting and retaining talented employees is crucial for high-performing organizations. As younger professionals enter the workplace, the call for workplace well-being has reached a fever pitch. A strong focus on belonging can be a vital tool in creating cultures where new professionals want to work.

Brand reputation is also important in attracting the best talent. Prospective job candidates can quickly assess an organization's commitment to diversity-led initiatives based on what they see and hear on social media and other avenues that have made communication more open. A culture-centric workplace that prioritizes inclusion is not only appealing to potential hires, but also plays a significant role in retaining the most talented current employees.

High turnover wastes an inordinate amount of time and money. Talent managers have estimated that it can take up to two years for new employees to reach full productivity in the knowledge economy. Depending on the role, filling a position that someone left based on poor culture fit could easily cost multiple six figures in running a new search and waiting for the new employee to work at their peak.

Cultivating an inclusive culture is also an essential strategy for protecting your company from employee complaints and accusations of unfair or discriminatory practices. For example, failing to use inclusive language can lead to a hostile work environment and potential discrimination complaints. Handling such incidents can be costly, both in terms of finances and reputation.

The U.S. population is becoming increasingly diverse, and younger generations are more likely to prioritize well-being and belonging in the workplace. Moreover, older consumers still wield significant purchasing power, and many individuals are working well into their retirement years. Organizations need to adapt to these powerful demographic shifts. Embracing inclusive leadership not only future-proofs your organization but also ensures that it remains agile, open to transformative ideas, and a workplace of choice for professionals of all ages.

Increasingly, inclusive leaders are also thinking about how their professional work can benefit themselves and their communities. "Strategic thinking, a skill revered in the boardroom," explains leadership development expert Eric Goodman, "is equally critical in crafting a fulfilling life." He views the melding of personal and professional in identifying "what success personally means to you and envisioning where you want to be in the future." Through "envisioning a desired future," he says, creates "an approach that helps you understand your strengths, weaknesses, opportunities, and threats along with the competitive landscape."

Since humans are so intensely hardwired for strategic thinking and goal-setting, an executive who works on self-awareness and inculcating culture via their leadership can literally "rewire the brain" by "strengthening neural pathways associated with planning, decision-making, and resilience." In other words, the skills that make you a better professional in the workplace are going to also naturally make you a better family member, parent, friend, and community leader.

MEASURING AND TRACKING PROGRESS

At any level of leadership—be it C-suite executives, middle managers, or emerging leaders—inclusive leadership can unlock transformative power through their teams. Inclusive leaders create environments where every individual feels valued, heard, and empowered. This inclusivity acts as a catalyst, igniting the flames of creativity, innovation, and collaboration. When diverse voices converge, solutions become holistic, strategies become comprehensive, and outcomes become extraordinary.

Consider a middle manager leading a team comprising individuals from various backgrounds. By weaving inclusive practices into their leadership fabric, this manager encourages each team member to contribute their unique insights. The result? A tapestry of ideas that far exceeds what any individual mind could conceive. It's this kind of collective genius that propels organizations toward their zenith.

Inclusive leadership ensures equitable treatment for all employees. Leaders at every level must embrace the responsibility of seeing that each team member has equal opportunities to succeed. This doesn't mean treating everyone the same; rather, it entails recognizing individual needs and tailoring support accordingly.

Imagine a senior executive overseeing a global team. Viewing the group through an inclusive leadership lens reveals that different team members might require varied types of support based on their cultural contexts, personal circumstances, and aspirations. By providing tailored guidance, this leader empowers every team member to excel.

Even in times of economic uncertainty, organizations with inclusive cultures perform better. Research, such as a study from Great Places to Work, reveals that companies with inclusive cultures outperform the S&P 500. The secret lies in the ability to create an environment where every employee is comfortable contributing their best work and original ideas. High-performing teams, guided by inclusive leaders, bring diverse perspectives to the table, driving innovation, efficiency, and quicker, better decision-making.

As McDonagh and Fitzsimons explain, gender imbalance on its own is a critical measure preventing organizations from realizing their full economic potential. Their research aligns with what we tell executives: "The more women on the board, the healthier your company will be." According to McDonagh and Fitzsimons, "Promoting and supporting women in senior roles must become a priority for every company's senior leadership. It should be core business. Every senior leader must tackle the cultures and practices which exclude talented women. If you look around your boardroom table and see too few, or even zero, women, then it is your responsibility to do something about it."

INCLUSIVE LEADERSHIP: IMPACT, TRANSFORMATION, AND BEYOND

The glue that holds great teams together is leadership transformed to meet the needs of people across the workplace. As the expectations of businesses and corporate leaders change and the demands increase for organizations to take a stance on societal topics and issues, how we define "leadership" must continue to evolve. Leaders cannot afford to be left behind as society continues to transform at breakneck speed.

Whether you're trying to win a championship, conduct an orchestra, or drive profits, you'll only succeed if you invest in leaders who can assemble and optimize great teams. The key to inclusive leadership is building a culture where teams uncover how each person contributes to the whole, including knowing their strengths and weaknesses, and appreciating their unique contributions.

The knowledge economy ebbs and flows on innovation spurred by talented people who identify issues and challenges and set out to rectify them. Thus, how people *feel* about an organization and its leadership team is essential in charting its march toward success. Imagine a work world that is recalibrated toward building and sustaining culture. Boards might then ask leaders: "Can you build a trusting culture that employees view as authentic and true to the spirit of your organization?"

Now, many employees are already empowered to ask similarly direct questions about a leader's ability to lead in a people-centric way. There must be a clear line between an executive's words and actions, living up to the organization's mission and vision. When there is a misalignment, talented people are going to walk out the door—virtually or physically—and find another opportunity, most likely with the competition.

The move into the C-suite, particularly for the CEO, is complex. Most people have little or no experience with the total accountability that is at the CEO's doorstep. We have counseled and coached many leaders who feel they could move into the C-Suite, but they haven't really thought deeply about the emotional temperament that it takes for that level of responsibility.

Aspiring leaders often don't realize that as a C-Suite executive, people are constantly misinterpreting your words and language in nearly every sentence you say. And, the emotive pull intensifies when you consider that you wake up each day with someone legitimately angry or upset at you because of a decision you made—every single day of your working life.

Let's be blunt—the so-called "soft skills" have not traditionally been the strong suit for many leaders. It's ironic that the aspect of leadership that has been least developed has become the most critical in this new era. The power in this new brand of strategic management is that the opportunity to learn and build out skills leads to limitless opportunity.

Putting essential elements into the garden—*well-being, trust, resilience, empathy, equity,* and *belonging*—the inclusive leader can create and build a sustainable organization that is hyper-focused on the fundamental business principles that matter, ranging from creativity and collaboration to innovation and problem-solving. In a culture-centric workplace, employees understand how belonging makes them perform better together and how trust leads to new ideas. And, perhaps most importantly, all employees are welcome and respected, based on what they bring to their roles.

By respecting each individual's identity and perspective, inclusive leaders build environments where every team member feels a meaningful sense of belonging and value to the collective mission. The result? Stronger, more cohesive teams that consistently exceed expectations.

In yet another irony, inclusive leaders actually increase their authority by being more open to their colleagues. They become more influential by building psychological safety and fostering a respectful environment that judges people on talent and teamwork, rather than where they went to school or how often they work in the office. An inclusive leader is a unifying voice and also a role model for how successful organizations operate in the global marketplace.

Leaders do not have unlimited power, but they can wield the power they have in an inclusive fashion. Getting people and teams focused on success means that you can only focus on two to three items at a time. People assume that a single, great person can move mountains to achieve greatness. We lived with this false image for decades.

In reality, it is not about the C-Suite leader, it's about the team that the leader assembles. You have the opportunity to select, mentor, train, and build up the team that is going to lead into the future. As a result, leaders are focused on choosing teammates who have a high upside and have the potential to be outstanding tomorrow. As a C-Suite leader, if you get that part wrong, then you might still be able to build a successful business, but it won't be the kind of organization that can change the world.

We have seen firsthand—with clients and across our own career journeys—that inclusive leaders want to build organizations filled with engaged employees who are ready to win in the marketplace. To achieve that end, they need to establish workplace excellence. Whether it is from an ESG perspective or just creating better collaboration, innovation, and profitability, we feel that businesses can benefit people and the planet, while also being profitable.

The new economy calls for a different approach to leadership that is focused on building culture-centric organizations that can make significant positive impacts on the world. We realize that doing anything to change the world isn't easy, but you have to confront the challenge head-on. We're convinced that we can change the world and inclusive leadership is the answer.

EXERCISES

Reflections

As you prepare for your inclusive leadership journey, it is imperative to turn the theoretical into the practical. Inclusive leadership demands a thorough engagement with its people-first principles and requires that executives internalize its critical tenets of communication, collaboration, self-awareness, cultural intelligence, capability, growth, and reliability. This reflection turns theory into action by weaving concepts into the foundation of organizational strategy.

Inclusive leaders—actively contemplating these fundamentals—create a more equitable and trustworthy workplace. They drive their organizations toward innovation and enduring success. Consider all that you've learned as you address these prompts:

1. Imagine you're mentoring a junior colleague on their journey toward inclusive leadership. What advice and guidance would you provide to help them develop these skills?

2. Considering what you have learned about inclusive leadership, what tactics or ideas can you implement immediately? What impact do you expect this to have for you personally and for your team?

3. Reflecting on the tenets of inclusive leadership, how will you use its principles this quarter to enhance your personal leadership style? What impact do you want to see on the teams you lead?

4. Which inclusive leadership competency most needs your attention? What steps will you take to enhance that competency? What specific actions will you take to improve your team's ability to collaborate more effectively?

SUPPLEMENTAL INFORMATION

APPENDIX I

The TDM LeaderView™ Inclusive Leadership Competencies

High-performing teams have the potential to increase sales, improve employee engagement, improve customer satisfaction, optimize product quality and more. Yet, leaders don't have the data and insights they need to make their teams more effective. They need a tool that will help them work better together as a team, which in turn, benefits the entire organization.

TDM LeaderView harnesses the full power of leadership teams in **ACT**ion (Assess-Coach-Train model). The result is better relationships and collaboration within leadership teams, so they can maximize their collective strengths and abilities.

With LeaderView, leadership teams will identify, build, and sustain the following seven core competencies, which are needed to navigate change, cultivate workplace belonging and well-being, enhance productivity, and spur innovation.

1. **Communication**

Defined—Communication, based on a culture of candor, is at the heart of team success and builds stronger relationships, fosters collaborative teamwork across function areas, and gets to critical conversations faster and more efficiently.

Demonstrated—Inclusive communication is delivered and received in a transparent, honest, and credible way that fosters trust. This is accomplished through practices such as active listening, checking for understanding, seeking feedback, and adapting communication styles when needed.

Developed—Stronger communication enables leaders to engage with stakeholders organization-wide, leading to persuasive, inspiring, and clear messaging. Credible and authentic communication nurtures trust, speeds the adoption of new ideas, and strengthens teams. This competency is the cornerstone for creating a collaborative culture that embraces critical feedback and enables teams to achieve better outcomes faster.

2. Collaboration

Defined—A collaborative culture not only invites others to participate in idea generation, but also encourages questions, dialogue, and even dissent. Unlike a group of individuals attempting to go it alone, strong cohesive teams have access to data that goes beyond what one person can know.

Demonstrated—Truly collaborative leaders nurture psychologically safe workplaces and teams where ambiguity is not feared and conflicting ideas are welcomed. Within this safe space, diverse talents are cultivated through open-mindedness and active listening, reinforcing a profound sense of belonging and individual contribution to the team's collective mission—even in the face of healthy tension. By acting as a facilitator and asking questions, inclusive leaders can create an environment where teams collaborate and solve issues together.

Developed—At the executive level, effective collaboration creates a sense of unity among leaders, empowering them to make business decisions quickly, while also ensuring that the company adheres and abides by its mission and values. When this culture is at the core, the executive team can strategically address issues as a single, cohesive force. Ultimately, inclusive leadership becomes the fabric of a culture-centric leadership team and steers the organization toward its goals with unparalleled synergy.

3. Capability

Defined—Capability is the proficient use of a leader's skills, knowledge, and behaviors to elevate team performance and achieve business outcomes. A capable leader is someone who naturally stands out, not only for their expertise, but for their ability to make everyone around them better

Demonstrated—Capable leaders demonstrate excellence in individual skills, while simultaneously fostering supportive, dynamic team environments that improve the efficiency of business processes. Leaders who display capability are goal-oriented and look for ways to link team achievement to company objectives. They effectively delegate, implement out-of-the-box solutions to problem-solving, encourage team development and skill building, and lead effective meetings to foster a culture of excellence across the organization.

Developed—Capability is the bedrock upon which trust and respect are built among colleagues, employees, and clients. Capable leaders enable others to scale their efforts for greater collective impact and evolve with societal changes, client needs, and the ever-fluctuating economic landscape. Ultimately, capability empowers leaders to exceed the expectations of their colleagues, teams, boards, and customers, driving both personal and organizational growth.

4. **Growth Mindset**

Defined—Continuous growth is imperative for the success of executive teams and business outcomes; it allows leaders to leverage the thinking of diverse groups to drive innovation and evidence-based decision-making. Being a growth-oriented leader means actively fostering a culture of teamwork, critical thinking, and inclusion.

Demonstrated—A growth mindset demonstrates vulnerability, adaptability and resilience. Through sharing experiences and knowledge, being transparent about mistakes, and recovering with confidence, an inclusive leader inspires their team to do the same, thereby creating a stronger leadership team across organizational roles and responsibilities. Maintaining tenacity in the face of risk and change empowers teams to confidently grow and innovate.

Developed—Promoting a growth mindset will not only improve the efficiency and productivity of your team, but the attitude will also feed an inclusive workplace culture. By engaging in ongoing learning and discovery, organizations are able to align on the pulse of customer needs and behaviors, while also fostering staff development. Leaders with a growth mindset are better prepared to address challenges, capitalize on new opportunities, and drive continuous improvement. A leader's ability to make bold decisions, venture into uncharted territory, and embrace uncertainty is imperative for expansion and innovation.

5. Cultural Intelligence

Defined—Cultural intelligence is the ability to empathetically respond to the human elements of business. It is the understanding that every person possesses a unique cultural frame that influences their worldview. In the context of an increasingly globalized business landscape, cultural intelligence is an indispensable trait for executive teams to enhance their effectiveness and leadership capabilities.

Demonstrated—Culturally intelligent leaders create opportunities for others to share difficult or uncomfortable information. They engage deeply to understand different cultures and customs. This understanding enables them to uncover unconscious bias, foster authentic connections, ask clarifying questions, and honor cultural differences to create a strong team environment.

Developed—Cultural intelligence equips executive teams with the tools to bridge cultural gaps; build strong, cohesive teams; and effectively navigate the complexities of the global business landscape. By nurturing cultural intelligence, executive teams unlock their full potential as leaders and create workplaces that are inclusive, diverse, and collaborative.

6. Reliability

Defined—In the pursuit of leadership excellence, the ability to consistently deliver results is paramount. A leader's reliability is the foundation for strong interpersonal relationships rooted in honesty and integrity. Inclusive leaders understand that trust is the currency of collaboration—reliability sustains it.

Demonstrated—Being a reliable leader means following through on commitments, while also ensuring your actions are fair and accurate. The hallmarks of reliable leaders include dependability, dedication to high-quality work, and adhering to timelines and budgets.

They recognize that the trust of colleagues and employees hinges on the consistent excellence of their output and the timely communication of it. This trust, in turn, is foundational for creating psychological safety and fostering respect in the workplace.

Developed—Reliability is essential in building high-trust cultures and high-performing businesses. By communicating transparently, prioritizing collaboration, and maintaining accountability as circumstances change, reliable leaders foster a culture of excellence among the team and across the organization.

7. Self-Awareness

Defined—Leaders who possess self-awareness are constantly attuned to the impact of their words and actions on others, allowing them to adapt and lead with greater efficacy. Self-aware leaders are acutely conscious of their thoughts, language, behaviors, and biases.

Demonstrated—Self-aware leaders commit to continuous learning through self-reflection, regular feedback from trusted advisers, and objective assessments. They harness the power of a supportive network, including family, friends, mentors, colleagues, and coaches. This network provides valuable guidance, development opportunities, and emotional support, allowing leaders to progress while understanding the outcomes of their actions.

Developed—Self-aware leaders are able to make more informed decisions, build trusting teams, and address the subtle influence of hidden biases on both personal interactions and the broader organization. A key benefit of self-awareness is a deep understanding of one's strengths and gaps, using internal and external feedback. Executives who embrace self-awareness nurture an environment where teams operate at peak efficiency and work collaboratively, thereby fostering personal and organizational growth. Self-awareness is also one of the most misunderstood principles in modern management. Most leaders view themselves as self-aware, but studies show that their assumptions are not shared with their employees. What seems like a fundamental is an area where most leaders can really dig in to make a difference with their teams and organizations.

APPENDIX II
11 Tips for Leading Effective and Inclusive Meetings

If you feel like you spend too much time in useless meetings, you're not alone. In a survey of 182 senior managers, 71% said meetings are unproductive and 65% said meetings are a barrier to getting work done. In order to maximize organizational efficiency, leaders need to ensure that every meeting counts. This means implementing strategies to make meetings more effective and inclusive for all attendees. Below are 11 tips for leading productive meetings.

1. **Provide structure.** Leaders should send meeting agendas in advance so attendees have time to prepare their thoughts and questions. This is especially crucial for neurodivergent professionals who may need additional time to process information. Meetings should also begin on time and end on time—or early. If the meeting is running long, consider setting up a follow-up meeting to finish the conversation.

2. **Establish meeting agreements.** Start any meeting by establishing a safe space where all attendees feel comfortable sharing their thoughts, ideas, and suggestions. Some recommended agreements include:

   - Be fully present. Put down your phone, leave the email, and give your attention to your colleagues.
   - Listen to understand. Absorb what your colleagues are saying instead of formulating your own response.
   - Assume good intentions. When topics are contentious or passions run high, remind yourself that everyone is trying to reach the best solution possible. Don't take it personally if someone disagrees with your opinion.
   - Make space, take space. Give plenty of time for others in the meeting to express their opinions, and speak up if you have a concern.
   - Take the lessons, leave the details. Respect the confidentiality of everyone in the meeting. Gossip and side conversations can kill trust within a team.
   - Ask questions to gain clarity. If you don't understand something, it's your responsibility to ask questions until you do. Miscommunication and misunderstandings waste time and energy.
   - Be open to new ideas and willing to admit mistakes.

3. **Invite people to speak up.** As a leader, you've probably noticed that some team members are frequent contributors, while others need encouragement to share their opinions. If you notice the conversation is leaving out certain voices, create opportunities for others to share. Be specific in the input you're looking for, so folks feel more confident participating. For instance, rather than asking simply "Brenda?" ask "Brenda, does that timeline seem reasonable to you?"

4. **Call out interruptions.** In order to ensure all voices are heard, it's critical that leaders call attention to and correct interruptions. Studies show that women are interrupted more frequently than men, and leaders should guard against this behavior to ensure equity. When you notice one colleague interrupting another, say something along the lines of "I'd like to hear Casey finish their thought" or "Wait one second, and I'll come back to you. Casey, would you please finish your thought?" If you notice that a specific team member interrupts frequently, you might pull them aside to address the issue directly.

5. **Give credit where credit is due.** Recognize each person's contributions to the team and the conversation by thanking individuals for their effort. For instance, you might give a shout-out in front of the full team, such as "Scott did a great job leading the discovery call with our client last week." Or, "Stephanie, that's a great idea. I'll be sure to bring that to the executive team." And, it's up to leaders to notice who suggests an idea first. If one person suggests an idea and another person later repeats it, say something like, "Yes, Stephanie just suggested that idea. It sounds like we are all in agreement."

6. **Use (and encourage) inclusive and thoughtful language.** Inclusive language has a large impact on employees' sense of day-to-day belonging. Be sure to implement inclusive language best practices into your own communications and encourage others to do the same. If you do hear someone use non-inclusive language, it's your job as a leader to correct them.

Aside from inclusive language, be mindful of how you phrase your responses to certain scenarios, as these responses can impact how people view future meetings. As an example, saying "Let's give everyone five minutes to join" can inadvertently contribute to a culture where people don't feel the need to show up to meetings on time. Meanwhile, saying you'll take something "offline" is usually interpreted as, "It's going nowhere." Instead, say something along the lines of "We definitely need to talk about that, but we don't have time today. Let's schedule another time this week to set up a longer conversation."

7. **Make meetings accessible.** Be sure that all attendees can fully access and participate in your meeting, whether virtual or in-person. For virtual meetings, enable closed captions and make sure audio and video outputs are high quality. For in-person meetings, make sure pathways are clear and rooms are navigable for those with mobility issues.

8. **Use various delivery methods.** Depending on the information you're discussing, it may be useful to display information in several formats. People have varying learning styles, and might interpret information best by listening to an explanation, reading a text, or looking at charts. For instance, if you're discussing earnings for the quarter, this information should be delivered verbally and graphically.

9. **Provide space for follow-up questions and input.** As mentioned before, neurodivergent professionals may need more time to process information. Therefore, when you solicit questions and final thoughts at the end of the meeting, they may not be ready to share. If an employee comes to you with additional input a few hours or days after the meeting, be sure to consider what they have to say.

10. **Send meeting minutes.** After meetings, provide attendees with a record of key discussion items, timelines, assigned tasks, and decisions made. This helps attendees remember the information and also provides helpful reference for those unable to attend.

11. **Only hold necessary meetings.** If you're like most professionals, odds are you've sat through a meeting only to leave thinking "That could have been an email." As a leader, make sure you're utilizing your employee's time wisely and only calling necessary meetings. Meetings are critical for certain conversations, such as brainstorming sessions or employee reviews; but if a status update can be quickly relayed via email, opt for digital communication.

Making sure your meetings are effective and inclusive can save your company time and money by making every meeting productive and useful for attendees. Instead of wasting time, create meetings that foster innovation and problem solving.

APPENDIX III
Build Better Hybrid and Remote Teams—15 Practical Tips for the New Workplace

The office looks a lot different today, after the pandemic caused organizations worldwide to rethink how and where work gets done. Remote work shifted from being an emergency tactic to business-as-usual for millions of people. Employees loved the flexibility and companies didn't have to maintain expensive office space. But the shift to remote work had unintended consequences for people managers and team leaders. It's harder to build team cohesion when colleagues aren't physically together, and it's challenging to manage virtual or hybrid teams.

As quickly as the office environment changed, supervisors suddenly had to navigate communication challenges and proximity bias. Leaders seldom explicitly state that they prefer in-person workers. Rather, there are small inequities that persist, where in-person workers are given more opportunities or more favorable reviews than remote workers. In fact, one recent study found that remote employees are less likely to be promoted than employees who come into the office, despite being 15% more productive.

The good news is that organizations, leaders, and employees can take actions to mitigate bias so proximity doesn't play a role in performance evaluations, opportunity, and access. Here are 15 practical tips for building better remote teams:

For Companies

- **Make all meetings accessible**: Whether it's a weekly team meeting, a brainstorm session, or a quick birthday celebration, all office meetings and events should have a dial-in option for remote employees. All employees, even those in-office, should log into the virtual platform.
- **Encourage virtual communication**: Use Slack, Teams, or another messaging platform for teamwide decision-making and chatter, so it becomes the hub for communication. This assures that any informal decisions or teamwide plans are made with the input and participation of remote employees.
- **Plan events so all employees can attend**: If remote employees come to the office occasionally, plan large meetings and team-building events for days when everyone is present.
- **Provide a travel budget**: If you have out-of-town employees, cover the costs of their travel to the office, so they can be present for company-wide events, collaborative projects, or team training.

- **Hold weekly check-ins**: Schedule formal, team-wide meetings where all members report on what they are working on. This allows managers to understand each person's contributions, gives in-office employees a sense of what remote employees are working on, and vice versa.

For Managers

- **Manage performance based on outcomes**: Managers can often see in-office employees working in a way that they cannot easily observe remote employees. In order to be more equitable in evaluating performance, managers should base reviews on results.
- **Build trust and togetherness**: Leaders can increase trust by role modeling four key characteristics: reliability, acceptance, openness, and authenticity. These traits, when enacted by the whole team, increase camaraderie, collaboration, and inclusion.
- **Increase team engagement**: Zoom fatigue is real, but video calls might be the only opportunities remote employees have to engage with the rest of the team. Make sure to keep meetings engaging and encourage full participation, so that remote employees don't feel excluded. Enable less verbal members of the team to participate through features like chat to create equity in soliciting input.
- **Encourage team problem-solving**: Encouraging team members to utilize each other as resources increases collaboration and innovation. Playing to the strengths of each team member makes the team more effective.
- **Mirror in-office activities remotely**: If your office puts on social events such as happy hours, monthly lunches, or birthday celebrations, do your best to mirror these in a remote way. For example, if you have a quarterly meeting with lunch provided, send your remote employees a Doordash or UberEats gift card.
- **Check in often**: It's easy for managers to catch direct reports in the hallway or break room for informal status updates. It's harder for managers to know what remote employees are working on every day.

For Employees

- **Turn on the camera**: Remote workers can mitigate bias against them by increasing their visibility, simply by turning on the camera for as many meetings as possible. There are many reasons to keep the camera off, so if you need to prioritize which meetings to be on for, do so.

- **Don't rely solely on text-based communication**: While text messaging may be the default and quickest way to communicate, consider changing it up with voice memos or quick video calls.
- **Advocate for your own professional development**: It is easy for in-office employees to gain informal mentoring or access to local professional development opportunities. Remote employees need to be intentional about seeking out these moments.
- **Offer solutions and reminders**: Although remote work has grown considerably in the last few years, companies are still figuring out how to get it right. For instance, did your supervisor leave off a dial-in line for your team meeting? If so, gently remind them to add one. Did HR hand out company-branded T-shirts at the office? Ask if they can mail you one. It's important that you speak up so that others know how you want to be included.

Remote work allows companies to spend less on office space, retain employees who might otherwise quit, attract talent from a wide geographic area, and recruit more diverse job candidates.

APPENDIX IV
C-Suite AI Guide—5 Actionable Steps to Spearhead Strategy and Implementation

When it comes to Artificial Intelligence (AI), there is an influx of new information coming to light each day. However, digging into the news and reports reveals much that is conflicting and confusing. With the global hype machine on overdrive, how is a senior leader to figure out what is meaningful versus what's hyperbole?

Looking at recent studies of what's on the CEO's mind provides little clarity—except, perhaps, to reveal the full-on existential crises most executives are living. The recent PwC Global CEO Survey reveals the dilemma senior leaders face:

- 45% are "not confident that their companies would survive more than a decade on their current path."
- CEOs believe AI will lead to "huge productivity benefits," but only 32% have broadly adopted it.

In other words, CEOs realize they need to change their organizations as soon as possible in order to remain sustainable. They also view AI as a key driver in creating the organization of the future. Yet, many people are fearful that companies are moving too fast without adequately addressing what these tools will do both to and for us.

There are many reasons for hesitation, but many of these are human-centered factors, ranging from the cost associated with upskilling and reskilling employees to outright fear of how an AI-dominant future will upend people's lives. These types of obstacles are being navigated while executives also attempt to balance how AI can bring short- and long-term efficiency gains. Then, there's the elephant in the room—getting the entire company to navigate the deep strategic moves it will need to unlock AI's full growth potential.

Driving AI Strategy Today

The first move every CEO must make is to assess the current state by asking a straightforward question: "Where are we today on our AI journey?" The primary consideration is to establish a baseline on current AI initiatives, understand projects that have an AI component, and evaluate the company's AI maturity level. Based on the PwC poll results with some 70% of organizations yet to implement AI, you might find that your organization hasn't yet begun or is only in its nascent stage.

No matter where you are right now, the second consideration is to ask your leadership team, "What quick efficiency gains can AI bring right now?" Whether potential wins are based on personal use or successes across teams, these benefits lay the foundation for more significant transformations.

These two initial questions will provide context and signal to your executive team that AI is a priority. What you learn can then be used to create the foundation for AI implementation.

5 Actionable Steps Toward An AI Strategy

AI initiatives are going to take decisive leadership from the top. CEOs should consider the following strategic moves to position their organizations for success:

1. **Comprehensive AI Readiness Assessment**: Initiate an organization-wide assessment to gauge readiness, building on the outcomes from discussion with your leadership team members. Evaluate the existing technological infrastructure, data quality and your employees' skill sets. Identify areas where AI can be seamlessly integrated to enhance efficiency, customer experiences and overall business outcomes.

2. **Establish a Cross-Functional AI Task Force**: Integrate from the start by creating a task force from various departments, including IT, data science, operations, marketing and legal. Foster collaboration to ensure a holistic approach to AI implementation. Supercharge their efforts by aligning AI initiatives with business goals, while facilitating communication across different functions.

3. **Invest in Employee Training and Upskilling**: Prioritize employee training programs to upskill your teams in AI-related technologies, data analytics and machine learning. Promote a culture of continuous growth to prepare your organization.

4. **Implement Ethical AI Guidelines**: Acknowledge the ethical considerations associated with AI and establish clear guidelines for responsible AI usage. Ensure transparency in AI algorithms, work to mitigate biases and prioritize data privacy. Communicate these guidelines across the organization to build trust among employees, customers and other stakeholders.

5. **Start with Small, Strategic AI Pilots**: Launch small-scale, strategic pilot projects to test AI applications in real-world scenarios. These programs enable your teams to learn, adapt and measure analytics before scaling up. Identify low-risk, high-impact

areas where AI can deliver immediate value. Use these pilot projects as learning opportunities for your teams.

Understanding and making sense of AI as a CEO involves a holistic approach that combines strategic evaluation, stakeholder engagement, ethical considerations and a commitment to ongoing learning. A comprehensive perspective enables you to navigate the complexities of AI with confidence, while simultaneously ensuring that your organization harnesses AI's full potential for growth and innovation.

WORKS REFERENCED

Alexander, Kerri. "Ava DuVernay." National Women's History Museum. https://www.womenshistory.org/education-resources/biographies/ava-duvernay

Arline, Trey. "DEI Specialist Discusses How Investing in Inclusive Technology and Mentorship Helps Long-Term Business Growth." October 14, 2022. *Senior Executive.* https://seniorexecutive.com/dei-specialist-discusses-how-investing-in-inclusive-technology-and-mentorship-helps-long-term-business-growth/

Boskamp, Elsie. "35+ Compelling Workplace Collaboration Statistics: The Importance of Teamwork." July 2023. Zippia. https://www.zippia.com/advice/workplace-collaboration-statistics/

Bourke, Julia & Titus, Andrea. "Why Inclusive Leaders Are Good for Organizations, and How to Become One." March 2019. *Harvard Business Review.* https://hbr.org/2019/03/why-inclusive-leaders-are-good-for-organizations-and-how-to-become-one

Breeden, Alice, Gailey, Rose, Johnston, Ian, & Rankine, Kate. "Getting on Board with Culture." 2022. Keidrick & Struggles. https://www.heidrick.com/-/media/heidrickcom/publications-and-reports/getting-on-board-with-culture_final.pdf

Brodo, Robert. "The Direct Link Between Psychological Safety and Business Results." May 3, 2022. Advantexe Blog. https://www.advantexe.com/blog/the-direct-link-between-psychological-safety-and-business-results

Carr, Evan, Reece, Andrew, Kellerman, Gabriella, & Robichaux, Alexi. "The Value of Belonging at Work." December 2019. *Harvard Business Review.* https://hbr.org/2019/12/the-value-of-belonging-at-work

Cisco, "Inclusive Communities." 2024. Cisco Systems, Inc. https://www.cisco.com/c/en/us/about/careers/we-are-cisco/inclusive-communities.html

———. "FY23 Purpose Report: The Power of Purpose." 2024. Cisco Systems, Inc. https://www.cisco.com/c/dam/m/en_us/about/csr/esg-hub/_pdf/purpose-report-2023.pdf

Cloverpop, "Hacking Diversity with Inclusive Decision-Making." September 2017. https://www.cloverpop.com/hubfs/Whitepapers/Cloverpop_Hacking_Diversity_Inclusive_Decision_Making_White_Paper.pdf

DeMattia, Adam. "A Mature Approach to Diversity, Equity, and Inclusion Delivers Real Results." March 2023. Enterprise Strategy Group. https://d1.awsstatic.com/executive-insights/en_US/esgamatureapproachtoDEI.pdf

De Smet, Aaron, Gast, Arne, Lavoie, Johanne, & Lurie, Michael. "New Leadership for a New Era of Thriving Organizations." May 2023. McKinsey & Company. https://www.mckinsey.com/capabilities/people-and-organizational-performance/our-insights/new-leadership-for-a-new-era-of-thriving-organizations

Erb, Marcus & Yoshimoto, Catherine. "Treating Employees Well Led to Higher Stock Prices During the Pandemic." August 2021. Great Place to Work. https://www.greatplacetowork.com/resources/blog/treating-employees-well-led-to-higher-stock-prices-during-the-pandemic

Eurich, Tasha. "Working with People Who Aren't Self-Aware." October 2018. *Harvard Business Review*. https://hbr.org/2018/10/working-with-people-who-arent-self-aware

Fankli, "9 Statistics that Link Employee Engagement and Performance." Frankli. https://www.frankli.io/post/connecting-employee-engagement-and-performance

Gallup, "State of the Global Workplace: 2023 Report." 2023. Gallup. https://www.gallup.com/workplace/349484/state-of-the-global-workplace.aspx#ite-506924

Haden, Jeff. "Bosses Beware: Research Shows You're Less Likely to Promote Remote Workers." September 2021. *Inc.* https://www.inc.com/jeff-haden/research-shows-youre-less-likely-to-promote-remote-workers.html

Hadley, Constance & Eun, Eunice. "Stop the Meeting Madness." July-August 2017. *Harvard Business Review*. https://hbr.org/2017/07/stop-the-meeting-madness

Hampton, Chloe. "Unhappy Workers Cost US Firms $1.9 Trillion." January 2024. Bloomberg. https://www.bloomberg.com/news/articles/2024-01-23/unhappy-at-work-quit-quitting-costs-us-1-9-trillion-in-productivity

Harter, Jim. "Employee Engagement vs. Employee Satisfaction and Organizational Culture." August 13, 2022. Gallup. https://www.gallup.com/workplace/236366/right-culture-not-employee-satisfaction.aspx

Harvard Business Review Analytical Services, "The Business Case for Purpose." 2016. Harvard Business Review/EY Beacon Institute. https://assets.ey.com/content/dam/ey-sites/ey-com/en_gl/topics/digital/ey-the-business-case-for-purpose.pdf

Kawamoto, Dawn. "How Microsoft's Inclusive Hiring Practice Produces Concrete Results." April 2023. Human Resource Executive. https://hrexecutive.com/inclusive-hiring-practice-yields-concrete-results-for-microsoft

Kitterman, Ted. "5 Ways Workplace Culture Drives Business Profitability." February 2023. Great Place to Work. https://www.greatplacetowork.com/resources/blog/5-ways-workplace-culture-drives-business-profitability

Kitterman, Ted. "Why and How to Build Trust in the Workplace." January 2023. Great Place to Work. https://www.greatplacetowork.com/resources/blog/why-and-how-to-build-trust-in-the-workplace

Lorenzo, Rocío, Voigt, Nicole, Tsusaka, Miki, Krentz, Matt, & Abouzahr, Katie. "How Diverse Leadership Teams Boost Innovation." January 2018. Boston Consulting Group. https://www.bcg.com/publications/2018/how-diverse-leadership-teams-boost-innovation

McDonagh, Margaret and Lorna Fitzsimons. "Women Count 2022: The Role, Value, and Number of Female Executives in the FTSE 350." 2022. The Pipeline.

https://d2e9sck8yc9g7g.cloudfront.net/wp-content/uploads/2019/09/06103843/Women-Count-2022-FINAL.pdf

McKinsey & Company, "Diversity Matters Even More: The Case for Holistic Impact." November 2023. McKinsey & Company. https://www.mckinsey.com/featured-insights/diversity-and-inclusion/diversity-matters-even-more-the-case-for-holistic-impact

Meyer, Anna. "Companies with Diverse Boards Out Performed Their Peers During the Pandemic." July 2021. *Inc.* https://www.inc.com/anna-meyer/diversity-board-directors-covid-pandemic.html

Noll, Doug. "Leading From The C-Suite: Donald Thompson of The Diversity Movement on Five Things You Need To Be A Highly Effective C-Suite Executive." March 19, 2023. Authority Magazine. https://medium.com/authority-magazine/leading-from-the-c-suite-donald-thompson-of-the-diversity-movement-on-five-things-you-need-to-be-a-72685166d545

Plaut, Alison. "What is an ESG Rating?" October 2023. The Motley Fool. https://www.fool.com/terms/e/esg-rating

PwC, "Thriving in an Age of Continuous Reinvention." January 2024. PwC. https://www.pwc.com/gx/en/issues/c-suite-insights/ceo-survey.html

Ringel, Rae. "Please Stop Using These Phrases in Meetings." January 2022. *Harvard Business Review.* https://hbr.org/2022/01/please-stop-using-these-phrases-in-meetings

Smith, Christie & Turner, Stephanie. "The Radical Transformation of Diversity and Inclusion." 2015. Deloitte University. https://www2.deloitte.com/content/dam/Deloitte/us/Documents/about-deloitte/us-inclus-millennial-influence-120215.pdf

Starner, Tom. "Why ERGs Drive the Growth of Workplace Diversity, and Much More." October 2016. HR Dive. https://www.hrdive.com/news/why-ergs-drive-the-growth-of-workplace-diversity-and-much-more/427500

The Diversity Movement, "Ask the Expert: Building a Strong Culture of Belonging with Passion and Purpose." TDM Library. https://tdmlibrary.thediversitymovement.com/ask-the-expert-building-a-strong-culture-of-belonging-with-passion-and-purpose

The Diversity Movement, "Ask the Expert: Coaching Inclusive Leaders and Ending 'Imposter Syndrome.'" TDM Library. https://tdmlibrary.thediversitymovement.com/ask-the-expert-coaching-inclusive-leaders-and-ending-imposter-syndrome

The Diversity Movement, "What is Inclusive Language?" TDM Library. https://tdmlibrary.thediversitymovement.com/what-is-inclusive-language-3

Thompson, Donald. "Unlock Excellence with Inclusive Leadership: A CEO's Guide." February 19, 2024. *WRAL TechWire*. https://wraltechwire.com/2024/02/19/donald-thompson-unlock-excellence-with-inclusive-leadership-a-ceos-guide/

———. "How to be an Inclusive Leader: Four Execs Share their Secrets to Success." August 16, 2023. *WRAL TechWire*. https://wraltechwire.com/2023/08/16/how-to-be-an-inclusive-leader-four-execs-share-their-secrets-to-success/

Wigert, Ben & McFeely, Shane. "This Fixable Problem Costs U.S. Businesses $1 Trillion." March 2019. Gallup. https://www.gallup.com/workplace/247391/fixable-problem-costs-businesses-trillion.aspx

Williams, Andrew. "How Cisco's Commitment to DEI Helped It Keep One of Its Best Employees for 23 Years (and Counting!)." August 18, 2023. *3BL CSRwire*. https://www.csrwire.com/press_releases/781801-how-ciscos-commitment-dei-helped-it-keep-one-its-best-employees-23-years-and

Zak, Paul. "The Neuroscience of Trust." January-February 2017. *Harvard Business Review*. https://hbr.org/2017/01/the-neuroscience-of-trust#:~:text=Compared%20with%20people%20at%20low,lives%2C%2040%25%20less%20burnout

ACKNOWLEDGMENTS

We believe that the future of leadership on a global scale hinges upon the principles of inclusive leadership. Our inclination is reinforced by the dynamic business landscape, which grows more interconnected each moment.

For executives and emerging leaders who want to build sustainable success, this paradigm shift points toward a culture where people can be their authentic self, driven by passion, purpose, and a desire to change the world. This has certainly been our experience in being two of the co-founders of The Diversity Movement and has been validated since becoming part of the Workplace Options team, which serves 80 million customers around the world in more than 200 countries and territories.

The Inclusive Leadership Handbook is testament to the transformative power of a people-centered leadership style that places teamwork and collaboration at the heart of culture. We hope the information in the book and the prompts along the way helps you become a better inclusive leader.

From Don—

To all the individuals I have had the opportunity to lead, be led by, or watch their leadership from afar, I want to say thank you. I realize that my early leadership journey was full of missteps and I appreciate leading in a world where transformation can take place through hard work and resilience.

I have been fortunate to have parents who instilled in me a deep desire to chase my dreams. My parents were role models for resilience, a gift they passed down to me. They also enabled me to develop a lifelong love for competitive learning, which I view as foundational in my commitment to get better each day. My sister Amie is—and always will be—a source of pride. I am grateful for her friendship.

My children are adults now and I'm so happy to now see the world through their eyes. Moriah, Ciera, David, and Diana have been a great source of pride. My love for them drives me.

When I talk about inclusive leaders, I often have Grant Williard in mind. He has been my mentor and friend. Thanks also to his wife Laura. Their partnership and marriage has been an inspiration.

There are a host of others who have helped me, not only with this book, but in clarifying and validating my thoughts about inclusive leadership. They include my teammates and colleagues at The Diversity Movement, particularly our Co-founders: Jackie Ferguson, Kurt Merriweather, Kristie Davis, Sharon Delaney McCloud, and Kaela Sosa. In addition, Andy DeRoin was instrumental in creating the TDM LeaderView methodology. I would also like to thank Amber Keister and Bob Batchelor for their editorial acumen.

Words can't express my gratitude for Jackie, my wife, partner, and soul mate. She is my rock and her love and support give me the strength to keep chasing my dreams. In fact, our relationship has been the closest thing I've experienced to a dream come true. Thank you Jackie!

From Kurt—
My introduction to leadership begins with my parents. They gave me a thirst for learning and created high standards and expectations, while exhibiting the patience to nurture the creative destruction needed to be an innovator. My attempts to fix everything with Scotch tape were a sight to see.

Kayla, Miles, Ellis, and Reese—You are my life's greatest work. I'm grateful that you challenge me to be a better person and leader, but most importantly, a better father. My greatest wish for you is that you continue to do the work you were destined to do and that you recognize that everything is possible for those who believe.

Valerie—You are the love of my life and have given my life meaning and purpose. The things I have accomplished are only possible because of you. You are my life's greatest blessing. I am because you are.

My professional life has been shaped by many organizations. One of the most important is the National Society of Black Engineers (NSBE). My role as Chapter President at The Ohio State University and then serving as a founding member of the Cincinnati alumni chapter were career defining opportunities for me.

My path to leadership has had many influences, including: Milton Anderson, Jay Crosby, Dean Minnie McGee, Ruby Smith, Robert Scott, Toby Spurlock, Kathy Lane, Bob Merriweather, Kirk Law, Greg Estes, Louise Ledeen, Jim Denney, Gabe Vehovsky, Drew Wilson, Grant Williard, and Todd Merriweather. I picked up leadership nuggets from all of you. Some of the lessons you taught were intentional. Others I learned by watching your model. The saying, "More is caught than taught" is definitely true. Thank you for pouring into me.

This book wouldn't have been possible without the best team that I have had the pleasure to work with. I'd like to thank Donald Thompson, Jackie Ferguson, Kristie Davis,

Jamie Ousterout, Shelley Willingham, and Kaela Sosa for being part of the founding team, which enabled us to test the inclusive leadership models that became The Diversity Movement. A special thanks goes to Bob Batchelor for helping the words and thoughts in this book sing.

ABOUT THE AUTHORS

DONALD THOMPSON, EY Entrepreneur Of The Year® 2023 SE Award winner, is a globally respected and sought-after business leader with a proven track record of success in growing firms. As a CEO, speaker, investor, advisor, entrepreneur, and executive coach, Thompson brings a wealth of experience and expertise to any organization. Don is CEO & Co-founder of The Diversity Movement, a Workplace Options company. A Certified Diversity Executive®, he is passionate about driving cultural transformation and delivering solid returns for employees and shareholders.

Under his leadership, The Diversity Movement has earned numerous accolades, including Inc. Magazine's 2021 Best in Business List in DE&I Advocacy and *Fast Company's* 2022 "world-changing ideas." In addition, Thompson is a three-time Inc. 5000 Fastest Growing Companies winner, named to the Forbes Next 1000 List, the Business North Carolina Power 100 List, and winner of the 2023 Independent Press Distinguished Favorite Book Award in Leadership.

Thompson serves on 12 boards across various industries, including marketing, health, and finance. He is also the author of the book *Underestimated: A CEO's Unlikely Path to Success* and hosts the podcast "High Octane Leadership in an Empathetic World," both of which provide valuable insights for business leaders. Thompson is a featured columnist, writing about leadership and culture-centric business transformation for *WRAL TechWire*, the Raleigh-Durham Research Triangle's most important business publication. With his competitive learning mindset, Thompson delivers actionable insights and is the perfect partner for anyone looking to take their business to the next level.

Follow him on LinkedIn for updates on news, events, and his podcast, or contact him at info@donaldthompson.com for executive coaching, speaking engagements, or DEI-related content. Working with Thompson is an opportunity to learn from one of the best and take your organization to new heights.

KURT MERRIWEATHER is co-founder and Vice President of Marketing and Innovation at The Diversity Movement, a Workplace Options Company. He developed the Micro-Videos technology platform named by *Fast Company* as a "World Changing Idea" and developed TDM Analytics, the platform used by TDM clients to collect over 1 million data points on organizational culture. Merriweather also led TDM's corporate development efforts, including the completion of a $1 million seed round and guided TDM to a successful exit with Workplace Options.

Merriweather is a sought-after advisor and speaker. He has served on the SXSW Pitch Advisory board and American Marketing Association (AMA) national nominating committee. He has been a Google for Startups pitch competition judge and mentor. Merriweather has facilitated courses at UNC Chapel Hill, advised research teams at NC State University, and mentored students at SKEMA Business School. He is passionate about addressing groups to help them leverage the link between DEI and innovation. Merriweather has delivered keynote sessions and executive workshops for Sustainable Brands, FujiFilm, NC Bio, AENC, Hitachi Energy, and NC Tech Association.

Merriweather's leadership experience at Discovery, AOL, and Procter & Gamble enables him to equip executives with the skills needed to lead inclusive teams. His recent work with organizations such as BAYADA Home Healthcare helped the company gain recognition from *Newsweek* as one of America's Greatest Workplaces for Diversity. In addition to his work at The Diversity Movement, Merriweather advises startup leadership teams on product and go-to-market strategy, inclusive team building, and innovation.

Merriweather holds a patent from his work at Warner Bros Discovery. He earned a B.S. in Electrical Engineering from The Ohio State University and a MBA from the Stanford Graduate School of Business. Kurt lives in Durham, North Carolina, with his wife Valerie. They are the proud parents of four amazing children.

the diversity movement
A Workplace Options Company

The Diversity Movement (TDM) partners with organizations to build and strengthen culture by tying real-world business outcomes to diversity, equity, and inclusion (DEI) initiatives. TDM's integrated approach enables leaders to create inclusive culture through the application of data-informed insight, award-winning content, technology, and DEI expertise. The result? Your organization benefits from better business outcomes delivered by more productive, innovative teams.

Putting Employees First - Employee Experience Solutions for the Future of Work

Building inclusive culture requires DEI to be integrated into the everyday work experience. TDM's award-winning tools and resources provide foundational learning, leadership development, and analytics needed to create inclusive and culture-centric organizations at scale.

- **MicroVideos** - DEI micro-learning journey delivered in the flow of work. Named a *Fast Company* "World Changing Idea"

- **TDM Library** - Multimedia content hub for one-stop DEI resources at a budget-friendly cost, like *The Harvard Business Review* for culture

- **TDM LeaderView** - Cultural competency assessment platform to create stronger leaders and leadership teams

- **Digital Courses** - Foundational courses for comprehensive DEI learning and compliance training

- **TDM Analytics** - Powered by 500,000 culture data points, Analytics helps organizations visualize DEI sentiment and provides benchmarks to guide next steps and track progress

In addition to our resources and tools, we provide customized consulting services to help you make progress along your DEI journey.

Taking the Next Step

Leaders turn to TDM for results — partnering on a difficult journey that demands expert guidance. We've helped thousands of leaders like you walk this road before. Your journey, our expertise — let's create a world-class inclusive culture together.

Contact
info@thediversitymovement.com
to get started.

TDM LeaderView™
Unlock High-Performance Leadership - Shape Team Success with Cultural Competency

Most leadership teams have underutilized capacity. Yet, leaders don't have the data and insights they need to make their teams better. You need a tool that will help you work better together as a team, benefiting the entire organization.

TDM LeaderView harnesses the full power of leadership teams in **ACT**ion (**A**ssess-**C**oach-**T**rain model). The result is better relationships and collaboration within leadership teams so they can maximize their collective strengths and abilities. With LeaderView, leadership teams will identify, build, and sustain the core competencies needed to navigate change, develop a culture of collaboration, and enhance productivity.

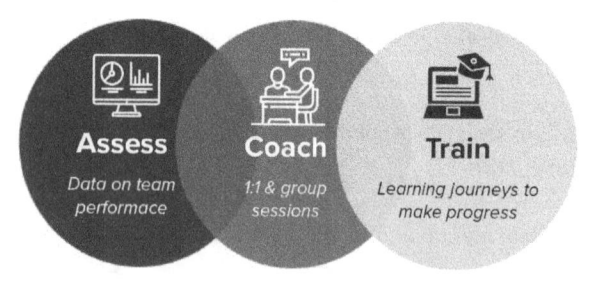

Inclusive Leadership Core Competencies

- Communication
- Collaboration
- Capability
- Growth Mindset
- Cultural Intelligence
- Reliability
- Self-Awareness

TDM Leadership Development ACT Model

- **Assess** — Data on team performance
- **Coach** — 1:1 & group sessions
- **Train** — Learning journeys to make progress

How LeaderView Works

The single-most critical component for whether executive teams succeed or fail is teamwork. LeaderView's focus on building a stronger team sets it apart from other individual-based assessments.

At a fraction of the cost of most leadership development solutions, LeaderView examines team strengths and gaps across **7 core competencies**. Identifying these areas enables teams to become tightly integrated and high-performing units. With personalized learning journeys backed by TDM's award-winning content and a visual dashboard to track progress, LeaderView provides tools and insights to establish culturally competent teams at scale following this proven methodology.

Taking the Next Step

Join the ranks of forward-thinking organizations that are harnessing the power of inclusive leadership to build stronger executive and managerial teams. Contact us today to learn how LeaderView can transform your team and drive lasting impact.

Contact info@thediversitymovement.com to get started.

Printed in the USA
CPSIA information can be obtained
at www.ICGtesting.com
LVHW060328150924
790966LV00005B/130